Returning to the Great Commission

Examining the Biblical Foundation and Effectiveness of Small Group Discipleship

Dr. Wanda Bolton-Davis

ISBN: 978-1-7343580-1-8

Dedication

I DEDICATE THIS book to my cherished gifts from God: my children, Kandis Levette, Denny Dwight, II, and Destiny DeYonne. Discipling you has been one of my greatest blessings.

To pastors, Bible teachers, seminary professors,
seminary students, lay leaders, those onboarding in ministry,
and every believer who is dedicated to making disciples

To Dr. Michael Wilkins of Talbot School of Theology,
for teaching and discipling me as a doctoral student

Acknowledgments
and Thank You

For your invaluable contribution

Yolanda Chambers

Dr. Joel Gregory, Ph.D.

Dr. LaSonja Flowers-Ivory

Dr. Charles Martin

Kandis Davis Reese

Kristie Savage

Linda Stubblefield

Table of Contents

Foreword
by Michael J. Wilkins, Ph.D.

IN JESUS Christ's final words to His followers we find His directive for the church throughout history. Every generation of the church stands under Jesus' powerful exhortation to "make disciples of all the nations" (Matt 28:19). In this famous "Great Commission," Jesus declares that His disciples were to make more of what He had made of them. In that sense, the Commission encapsulates Jesus' purpose for coming to earth. Jesus has come to inaugurate the kingdom of God on earth by bringing men and women into a saving and transformational relationship with Himself, which is called "discipleship to Jesus."

The structure of the Great Commission is well known to include one primary, central command, the imperative "make disciples," with three subordinate participles, "go," baptizing," and "teaching." Therefore, the imperative explains the central thrust of the commission, while the participles describe aspects of the process. Jesus' Great Commission implies more than securing salvation as His disciple. Implied in the imperative "make disciples" is both the call to and the process of growing as His disciple. Even as a person is called from among the nations to start life as a disciple, that person must in turn follow Jesus in discipleship through baptism and through obedience to His teaching. It is not enough simply to become a convert to Jesus; true conversion produces transformation. Without transformation there is what Wanda Bolton-Davis calls the "discipleship deficit."

Wanda Bolton-Davis clearly understands the significance of Jesus' Great Commission. It is a whole-life and life-long process. And it is a process that includes community. We are not in this process alone. We need other brothers and sisters who will encourage us, prod us along, comfort us, and share the load of the journey. Wanda Bolton-Davis provides a realistic method of developing community discipleship through small groups. The kind of small groups she envisions are those where we share life together, where realistic transformation occurs in the messy details of life. In small groups, disciples of Jesus grow in His image as they share personal, spiritual, and emotional transformation through the study of God's Word, Christian edification, and fellowship.

Wanda's careful guidance in this book will show how small groups can intentionally and strategically provide an environment for a life-transforming, ongoing, progressive path of spiritual growth with others who are on the same journey. Discipleship is a more comprehensive approach than simply attending church or participating in a class. Discipleship to Jesus involves a necessary relational aspect, where people engage in the Word together and have opportunity to do life together, creating an environment for transformation.

I had the privilege of leading a doctoral cohort on discipleship for more than three years in which Wanda participated. She was a wonderful member of the group. Her years of experience in the church and her close, personal walk with Jesus were an inspiration to all. She went through personal difficulties that were a true challenge for her, yet she never wavered in her commitment to Jesus's calling on her life. The principles that she lays out in this book have been clearly tested and lived out in Wanda's own walk with Jesus, in her personal relationships, and in her experience as a leader in the church. The culmination of her academic training resulted in a doctoral project entitled "Evaluating the Effectiveness of Small Group Discipleship."[1] That project has been carefully tested and now made practical in this book for the people of the church. Wanda has a depth of training in biblical studies that gives substance to her guidelines, and, at the same time, she is practical in her suggestions for implementation.

As she makes clear, community is created when individuals come together in small groups that foster trust, grace, humility, affirmation, and accountability in authentic relationships. But this isn't just inward-looking. Small groups encourage an outward-looking participation in the mission of God as participants learn to co-labor with God and join Him in His work to advance the kingdom of God for His glory. This is the challenge to return to the Great Commission through small group discipleship.

– Michael J. Wilkins, Ph.D., *Fuller Theological Seminary Distinguished Professor Emeritus of New Testament Language and Literature, Talbot School of Theology, Biola University* Author of *Following the Master: A Biblical Theology of Discipleship* (Zondervan) and *Matthew, NIVAC* (Zondervan).

---

[1]Wanda Bolton-Davis, "Evaluating the Effectiveness of Small Group Discipleship," DMin diss., Biola University Talbot School of Theology, 2015.

Preface

"Disciple them!" Those were the words I heard in my spirit over 20 years ago as I was praying for four young ladies. At that time, I had no idea what those words meant. Although I had accepted Christ at an early age and had been involved in church all my life, I had never experienced intentional discipleship.

For several weeks, I continued to pray, and the words persisted. I knew God was calling me to a purposeful relationship with these women. Without fully knowing what this relationship would entail, I reached out to each of them and proposed that we commit to meet with each other as a group, once per month, for one year. Each of them responded with excitement, confirming my proposal was exactly what they needed. I hung up the phone still not fully understanding what God wanted me to do with this group; but little did I know, it was more about what God wanted to do with all of us.

In January 2000 we had our first meeting, and we met the first Saturday of every month for a year. God amazed us all as we saw before our eyes how each of our lives were transformed as we studied the Word of God together, prayed together, cried together, talked and shared life experiences, and formed a bond that remains strong even today. We learned to know and experience God in ways we had never known or experienced Him before. Writing our lessons for our time together later led me to publish a discipleship workbook, *Victorious*

Disciples: A Guide to Christian Discipleship and Mentoring. Without any marketing, the small ministry I began with just four women, expanded to include men and women, small groups, and churches across the country. Whenever I think about it, I am humbled and stand in awe at God. However, through the years I have learned that what God called me to do over 20 years ago was nothing new. God merely called me to join Him in His work. He called me to return to His method of making disciples that He established over 2000 years ago. I simply obeyed. It was all in His power and for His glory. As a result, I committed my life's work to making disciples of Jesus Christ and training others to do the same.

In 2020 we saw something that we could have never imagined. The global pandemic of the coronavirus literally took us by storm, closing the doors of churches across the country, eliminating the assembling of believers, and preventing Christians from worshipping together in community. This shutdown brought us to the reality of the fact that the church is not in the building, but rather, the church resides within every believer. However, the pandemic brought about something even deeper than the closing of church doors. It revealed which churches had focused on congregants with membership status and which churches had prioritized making true, authentic disciples of Jesus Christ. For some churches, this reality determined their ability to survive this unprecedented time. It demonstrated whether the foundation of the local church was built on solid ground or sinking sand. Churches who had effectively made disciples, had developed people who recognized that their worship, walk, and witness was not limited to a place or a location. They understood they were called to a lifestyle that reflected Christ every day and everywhere. Indeed, the coronavirus pandemic placed the spotlight on the significance of true discipleship.

This book is for spiritual leaders and all believers. Now more than ever, church leaders, we are *called to make disciples*. We must deny ourselves, take up our cross, and follow Jesus (Matt. 16:24). Not only must we go deeper in our personal commitment to the Lord, but we must also commit to equip other believers to go deeper in their relationship with the Lord. As you read these pages, my prayer is that you will be encouraged, enlightened, informed, and if necessary, even convicted. May it ignite within you the passion to answer the call to make disciples. May your church become a place where you are strategic and intentional about producing true authentic disciples of Jesus Christ, who don't just go to church, but who become the church. I pray you will accept the invitation to *Return to the Great Commission*.

– Wanda Bolton-Davis

Introduction

THIS BOOK is the culmination of my doctoral project, "Evaluating the Effectiveness of Small Group Disciple-ship."[2] It addresses the problem of non-discipleship within the church, which has resulted in a disciple deficit within Christendom. This dilemma has created the need for churches to implement a discipleship strategy whereby church members are intentionally, consistently, and effectively discipled. To address this issue, I propose the ministry model of small group discipleship. Through my research, small group discipleship yielded favorable outcomes for participants in the areas of spiritual growth, a sense of community, and participation in the mission of God. This book will address each of these areas.

Chapter 1 examines the biblical and theological foundation for discipleship. It also addresses the concept of discipleship found in the Old Testament, while demonstrating Jesus' example and marked characteristics of discipleship in the New Testament. In Chapter 2, I address the spiritual problem of non-discipleship, non-discipleship Christianity, and the disciple deficit which has resulted. Chapter 3 examines some fundamental steps church leaders can take to address the problem of non-discipleship. In Chapter 4, I introduce the ministry model of small groups as an effective method of discipleship. Chapter 5 discusses how small groups impact spiritual growth and the importance of churches having spiritual growth outcomes. In Chapter 6, I cover how small groups form a greater sense of community, fostering belonging, accountability, and care. Chapter 7 is a reminder that what we do is all about the kingdom of God and looks at how small group discipleship involves people in the mission of God. Chapter 8 lays a solid foundation for small group discipleship and provides a template for developing a Spiritual Growth Path for ministry use. In Chapter 9, I provide practical steps regarding how to implement or enhance a discipleship ministry within the local church. Finally, chapter 10 presents us all with the challenge to return to the Great Commission, making disciples as Jesus modeled and instructed.

[2]Wanda Bolton-Davis, "Evaluating the Effectiveness of Small Group Discipleship," DMin diss., Biola University Talbot School of Theology, 2015.

CHAPTER ONE

Where It All Began:
The Bible and Discipleship

The Concept of Discipleship in the Old Testament

ALTHOUGH THE words *disciple* and *discipleship* do not appear as such in the Old Testament, there is clearly an abstract formation of master-teacher relationships interwoven throughout its pages. Michael Wilkins explains that there must be a clear distinction between discipleship terminology, which is not found in the Old Testament, and the concept of discipleship, which is clearly encountered in the Old Testament. Wilkins states,

> The relative absence of disciple terminology in the Old Testament should not be taken as a lack of the concept, and the type of concept needs to be delineated by the use of the terms in context as well as other evidences.[3]

By examining various relationships in the Old Testament, it becomes apparent that the conceptual idea of discipleship is present. The concept of discipleship in the Old Testament can be examined through the lenses of biblical covenants, tribal community, in the Greco-Roman world, during the Hellenistic Era, and within Judaism.

Biblical Covenant Relationships

God's nature is to be in relationship, and relationship involves covenant. Biblical discipleship can be more fully understood and appreciated when observed in light of Old Testament covenant relationships. Jonathan Lunde writes, "Each of the [Old Testament] covenants in its own way anticipates the establishment of the New Covenant described in Jeremiah 31:31-34."[4] God created humankind so that people could be in relationship with God and with each other. Since the beginning of humanity, discipleship was prefigured as God called His people to be in covenant relationship with Him. This calling is expressed in a pattern of divine initiative and human response manifested in the recurrent promise, "I will be your God, and you shall be my people." The relationship to which God called His people in the Old Testament not only included a covenant, but additionally, the response involved faith and obedience.

Wilkins asserts that discipleship relationships can be observed in the Old Testament on three levels. The first is on the national level, where a nation is called to be in relationship with God (Lev. 26:12).[5] Although God called Abraham, Isaac, and Jacob, the covenant He made with them was directed toward Israel as a people. Second, discipleship can be observed in the Old Testament between God and specific individuals such as Joshua (Num. 32:12), Caleb (Num. 32:12; Josh. 14:8-14), and David (1 Kings 14:8; 2 Sam. 2:7), who personalized the national covenant and individually followed God.[6] The third type of discipleship relationship observed in the Old Testament is discipleship within human relationships where individuals followed a great human teacher or master, such as Moses and Joshua (Num. 27:18-23) and Elijah and Elisha (2 Kings 2).[7]

In addition to observing covenant relationships in the Old Testament, four unique characteristics of the human discipleship relationships were displayed during ancient times. First, the relationship was oriented toward service. Second, both master and disciple were chosen by God to carry out God's work. Third, the relationships between the individuals were functionally related to crisis periods in Israel's history, and individuals were brought together for a specific purpose and for a specific time. Fourth, discipleship relationships during ancient times consisted of the master directing the disciple to God and not to himself, so that the disciple was ultimately following, serving, and walking with God.[8]

Tribal Community

The concept of discipleship is also seen in the Old Testament through tribal community through the people of Israel. The Old Testament has no specific theology of small group discipleship. However, reflections of discipleship are seen through tribal community, marital community, familial community, and friendship. The implementation of small groups is seen in Hebrew Scripture as Moses was encouraged by his father-in-law Jethro to appoint capable, God-fearing, and trustworthy men to oversee groups of thousands, hundreds, fifties, and tens, in order to serve the needs of the Hebrew people (Exod. 18:13-27).

These instructions were given to Moses after Jethro witnessed the overwhelming responsibility Moses encountered attending to the cares and concerns of so many people. Dividing into smaller groups was not uncommon for many tribal/nomadic people during that time. However, this strategy was unique for the Hebrew people because God had always provided for their daily needs, which made it unnecessary for them to break into small units to sustain themselves.[9] Therefore, this concept of smaller groups may have been new for the Israelites, but it proved to be effective. As a result, Israel began a leadership system divided into small groups, utilizing chosen and trustworthy leaders.

Discipleship in the Greco-Roman World

Discipleship becomes more visible in the Greco-Roman culture. Western civilization traces its roots back to Greece, which provided the foundation for the first democracy and advancements in math, science, art, architecture, literature, science, and philosophy. Greeks were known to be thinkers who laid the foundation for modern scientific thinking.

In his book, *The Complete Book of Discipleship*, Bill Hull explains that although Greek philosophers were confused about God (Acts 17:22-23), they insisted on passing on their polytheistic learning; they were "astute in passing on their confusion as they lived out discipleship and even created some of its language and technique."[10] Throughout this period, the term *mathetes* took on various meanings—from learner/apprentice, pupil/academician, and disciple/adherent. However, Wilkins states that the type of relationship was not defined by the meaning of the term *mathetes*; rather, it was the dynamic of the relationship and the aspect of commitment to the master that characterized the meaning of the term.[11] As a result, the characterization of the relationship gave context to the term, and this differed from relationship to relationship.

Discipleship During the Hellenistic Era

During the Hellenistic period when the New Testament was written, numerous relationships related to the term *mathetes* continued. However, the learning emphasis within the relationship decreased, and the focus shifted more toward the imitation of conduct. Paul R. Spikard and Kevin M. Cragg suggest that perhaps this emphasis was due to the changing culture created by the armies of Alexander the Great, where people were no longer part of a small-scale Greek city-state *(polis)*, but found themselves in a pluralistic society where many gods were worshiped.[12] As a result, there was a great need for moral guidance. Thus, relationships were clearly marked by a person who was a committed follower (disciple) of a great master or religious figure.[13]

Discipleship within Judaism

Discipleship within Judaism of the first century also involved many dynamics. Wilkins addresses five biblical and extrabiblical conceptions of discipleship within the world of Judaism of the first century. First, there were disciples of Israel's religious heritage.[14] This type of discipleship involved a personal commitment to a person who spoke for God, such as Moses. It also involved a commitment to Torah.

The second form of discipleship seen within Judaism was related to disciples within certain religious groups.[15] Wilkins asserts, "The various subgroups that existed within Judaism in the first century each had their own followers. Several of them could be described by master-disciple terminology."[16] Although ideally every Israelite followed God, there were those who were disciples of various subgroups within Judaism. Some of these include the Pharisees (Matt. 22:15-16; Mark 2:18; 22:16-17), who were students of law and tradition. They were committed to living out the law and traditions and today are known for their legalism. There were the scribes, who were official interpreters of the law. There was also an institutionalized formal educational system for aspiring rabbis whose followers focused on learning and practicing oral Torah.

The third conception of discipleship within the world of Judaism relates to those who were disciples of particular prophets.[17] Some of Israel's prophets had disciples. Isaiah indicated he had prophets (Is. 8:16). Elijah mentored Elisha (1 Kings 19:19-21). Elisha later taught the "sons of prophets" (2 Kings 2) and gave instructions to "the company of prophets" (2 Kings 4:38). Samuel ordered Saul to meet with "a procession of prophets" in preparation of Saul's appointment as king

(1 Sam. 10:5). Additionally, prophets appeared to have had a unique relationship with kings, such as with Isaiah and Hezekiah, Samuel with Saul, and Nathan with David.

It is apparent that many of the Old Testament prophets had followers. The New Testament mentions that John the Baptist had disciples (Matt. 9:14, 11:2, 14:12; Mark 2:18, Luke 11:1, 5:33, John 3:22-26; Acts 19:1-3). Andrew, Simon Peter's brother, was originally a follower of John the Baptist (John 1:35-41), and it is also likely that the other disciple of John the Baptist was John, the disciple whom Jesus loved, mentioned in John 1:35.

The fourth group that reflects a conception of discipleship during the ancient time of Judaism involves the disciples of the remnant of Israel.[18] This group includes the Qumran community who reflect the dynamic of discipleship in terms of imitation and community conviction. This group saw themselves as the "true" Israel as they isolated themselves to practice devotion to God and Torah, as taught by the Teacher of Righteousness. The Qumran community was organized by rank, and it is probable that the priests were those who studied Torah continually so that they could teach the other members.[19]

Lastly, there are the disciples of a Messianic Movement.[20] There were several different messianic movements in effect during the time of Jesus, and many followed Jesus for various reasons. There were those who were committed to His teaching, but many followed Him merely for His rising popularity and because they hoped for a king who would bring political peace and put Roman rule to an end. However, Jesus brought new meaning to the idea of discipleship. Jesus began to teach that the kingdom of God was near (Matt. 4:12-17; Mark 1:14-16), and shortly thereafter, He began to summon His followers who would soon be called His disciples (Matt. 4:18-22; Mark 1:16-20; 2:14; John 1:37-39, 43-46).

The calling of Jesus' disciples was not based upon their merit or abilities, but rather upon the basis of grace. Jesus chose twelve simple, unassuming men from Galilee, who had very limited means and no social status. Rather than consideration of material wealth or social standing, He desired men with humble hearts who would live a life of obedience to His Word.

Discipleship in the New Testament

Each of the Gospels give an account of Jesus' life, ministry, and His relationship with the disciples. Each author wrote from a different perspective and provide marked characteristics and theological foundations of discipleship, providing a guide for discipleship today. Distinct highlights are provided which help shape an understanding of Jesus' purpose in calling the disciples. Thus, the four Gospels provide a well-rounded view of what Jesus intended for discipleship to look like.

► *The Gospel of Matthew*

The gospel of Matthew gives a realistic picture for all Christians and demonstrates a general process of growth and spiritual development. Jesus is revealed as the effective teacher, and He identifies true disciples as those who understand His teaching (Matt. 13:51; 16:12; 17:13), are obedient to His teaching (Matt. 7:21, 24; 12:49-50), understand His parables (Matt. 13:51; 24:32), and are discipled in the ways of the kingdom (Matt. 13:52; 27:57). Conversion marks the beginning point of discipleship. Therefore, discipleship is for all believers, and there is no distinction between believers and disciples, although disciples may have various functions.[21]

► *The Foundation of Discipleship: The Great Commission*

Upon meeting the disciples in Galilee, Jesus makes an exceptional claim and gives the disciples an imperative assignment. He first claims all authority, rule, dominion, and jurisdiction, by stating that "all authority" in heaven and on earth has been given to me" (Matt. 28:18b). Then He charges the disciples to "go make disciples of all nations, baptizing them in the name of the Father and of the Son and of the Holy Spirit" (Matt. 28:19a). Jesus, who has been given complete authority by the Father, confers this authority to the disciples as He gives them their life assignment. It is because Jesus has plenary authority and can delegate power to whomever He wills that He confers the commission.[22] This commission was not only for the disciples of Jesus' day, but for every future disciple of Jesus as well. They were to go forth and carry the gospel throughout the world. Herein lies the implication that all Christians are called to be evangelists, spreading the gospel of Jesus Christ. The assignment of making the gospel known to the world is a task given to every believer.

For three years, the disciples had been in Jesus' constant presence and now, right before His ascension, He was commissioning them to carry on the work for which He had trained them (Mark 3:13-14). They were being deployed to do what they had been taught to do. Making disciples of "all nations" meant the gospel was not for the Jews only, but was also for the Gentiles. The partition between the Jews and Gentiles had now been broken, and the call to be and make disciples was for everyone who believed on Jesus' name (Mark 15:38; Eph. 2:14; Heb. 10:19-20).

By authority from heaven and not of man, they were to baptize in the name of the Father, and of the Son, and of the Holy Spirit. This baptism entailed more than the act of water immersion and external washing but involved being baptized into Christ—in His death and resurrection, and then being clothed with Him (Rom. 6:3, 1 Cor. 12:13, Gal. 3:27, Col. 2:12, 1 Pet. 3:21). This baptism symbolized a new identity with and in Christ.

In addition, Jesus' mandate to the disciples was to teach. The Great

Commission adds that believers should be "teaching them [new Christians] to obey everything I have commanded you" (Matt. 28:20a). These verses imply more than conversion alone; Jesus instructed the disciples to teach His followers to obey. He wanted them to do for others as He had done for them—teach them in word and deed. This involved giving instruction according to the whole counsel of God's Word so that followers of Jesus Christ might learn to live a life in obedience to His Word.

As believers are transformed by the Word of God, they have the responsibility to duplicate themselves in others, leading men and women in every part of the world to faith, baptism, and obedience to all of Christ's commands. Jesus taught the disciples and modeled the way before them (Matt. 5:2, Mark 11:17). Likewise, the disciples were to make disciples and teach them.

Jesus taught and set an example before the disciples. He trained them by word and deed, preparing them to be deployed. Along with the assignment that was now placed on the disciples' lives, Jesus provided the promise of His everlasting presence. Jesus said, "And surely I am with you always, to the very end of the age" (Matt. 28:20b). This promise has no expiration date—"until the end of the age"—and therefore, Jesus remains with every disciple today.

► The Gospel of Mark

In Mark, the disciples display difficulty in understanding the nature of Jesus' ministry and teaching (Mark 4:13, 35-41; 6:45-52; 7:17-18; and 8:14-21). They did not understand Jesus' true identity as the Son of God, His way of thinking, His practices, or the way of suffering. Jesus' view on discipleship was that of servanthood. Jesus taught, "If anyone wants to be first, he must be the very last, and the servant of all" (Mark 9:35; 10:43-45). Jesus emphatically taught that His disciples were not to be as the Gentile rulers who aspired to greatness, but that those who were the greatest in the kingdom would be servants. Jesus' teaching contrasted with what was esteemed as great in the Gentile world system. The greatness of the individual comes from the lowly place. Jesus Himself was an example of that.

Mark exposes the disciples' failures and uses this to instruct the community to think as God thinks, both about servanthood as well as suffering. To be a member of the kingdom of God was to be a servant, which meant suffering was inevitable and endured for the advantage of others and not for one's own gain. Although Jesus paid the price of death for us, the reality of sin exists, and suffering is inevitable. Jesus not only foretold His own suffering and death, but He made it known that suffering would be required and experienced by all who followed Him. Jesus said, "If anyone would come after me, he must deny himself and take up his cross and follow me" (Mark 8:34). Jesus made it clear that there would be a price for choosing to follow Him.

To deny oneself meant to let go of the natural inclination to seek personal gain, motivation, gratification, desires, and wants. It involved self-denial, in exchange for God's ways and purposes; to "take up His cross" involved absolute surrender. This includes putting to death your own life (Matt. 16:25) in order to gain it through Him.

Denying oneself meant to forget oneself, lose sight of oneself and one's interests; to "take up His cross" was to take up the cross of death; and to "follow Me" was to accompany another, taking the same road as another and fellowshipping with him along the road. For the disciple, these acts were to be a permanent attitude and practice of life.[23] In addition, suffering with and for Christ also meant that no suffering would be without meaning.

The Gospel of Luke

Luke points out that there were many who followed Jesus. Discipleship characterized those who were willing to count the cost, which meant sacrificing their own desires and making God the center of their faith (Luke 9:57-62; 10:25-37; 14:25-33). Counting the cost entailed detachment from anything that competed with one's commitment and loyalty to Jesus. Luke writes, "If anyone comes to me and does not hate his father and mother, his wife and children, his brothers and sisters—yes, even his own life—he cannot be my disciple" (Luke 14:26). Jesus was not demanding that His followers literally hate their families, but He was demanding complete loyalty, and He wanted His followers to consider what their allegiance to Him would cost them. Luke therefore puts emphasis on complete allegiance to Jesus, with the cost being one's life, the willingness to take up the Father's will on a daily basis (Luke 9:23).

Ultimately, disciples must give themselves totally to Jesus so that He may carry out the work of transforming them to reflect His image. Counting the cost not only meant showing love and mercy to others, but also, as Wilkins writes, "to count the cost meant to recognize that one entered into the life of discipleship through detachment from competing allegiances and through giving personal allegiance to Jesus as Master."[24] Counting the cost not only involved the initial sacrifice of becoming a disciple, but also the cost of remaining faithful.

The Gospel of John

The book of John expresses several fundamental characteristics of a disciple. Through abiding in Jesus' teaching, the disciples came to know Jesus through the display of love and knowing Him became evident in their actions. This is an example of how the inner transformation that occurs within every disciple will be exemplified externally.

The change that transpires in the heart of a believer will ultimately be demonstrated and displayed by their actions. Radical inward change bears visible external fruit.

Jesus said, "If you hold to my teaching, you are really my disciples. Then you will know the truth, and the truth will set you free" (John 8:31-32). Jesus made it known that mere belief in His teaching was not enough, but that His disciples had to follow and obey His teaching. Likewise, today, the adherence of one's life to Jesus' teaching is proof of the reality of their profession of faith. The continuance in Jesus' words reveals the sincerity or insincerity of one's faith. In other words, obedience is the acid test of a disciple. The commitment to abide in Christ is what makes the difference. Jesus speaks of abiding in Him in John 15, which provides a portrait of what a disciple looks like. Through the metaphor of a vineyard, we come to understand that Jesus is the vine, the Father is the vinedresser, and we are the branches. We learn there are several characteristics of a disciple:

1. A Disciple Abides in Christ through the Word and Prayer (vv. 3-7). To abide in Christ is to continue, dwell and endure in Him. Abiding involves a person's perpetually being united with Christ in heart, mind, and will. The believer is to remain attached to the vine, our life source, through the Word of God and prayer.

2. A Disciple Bears Much Fruit (v. 8). Fruit is the evidence that springs forth as a result of having remained connected to the vine. There are varying degrees of fruitfulness. The branches that bear no fruit are cut away, and others are purged so that they might be more fruitful. This truth is further demonstrated in the parable of the sower, where the growth of the seed that fell along the path, the rocky places, and the thorns, failed to compare to that which fell on good soil (Matt. 13). Jesus said, "This is to my Father's glory, that you bear much fruit,

showing yourselves to be my disciples" (John 15:8). Showing the love of God through obedience bears fruit, and fruit brings glory to God. Fruit that comes out of a person's obedient faith-union with Christ is the foundation of how Jesus brings glory to the Father. The apostle Paul defines the fruit of the Spirit as "love, joy, peace, patience, kindness, goodness, faithfulness, gentleness, and self-control. Against such things there is no law" (Gal. 5:22-23). This is what brings glory to God.

3. A Disciple Responds to God's Love in Obedience (vv. 9-10). A disciple remains in God's love by obeying His commands. The apostle John also states, "If anyone chooses to do God's will, he will find out whether my teaching comes from God or whether I speak on my own" (John 7:17). Obedience sets the disciple apart.

4. A Disciple Possesses Joy (v. 11). Christ has placed joy within every believer. It is to infuse everything we do. Like a nursing baby who receives nourishment from the mother, Jesus nourishes Christians with joy that only He can make complete.

5. A Disciple Loves Others as Christ Loves (vv. 12-13). A disciple's life is to be characterized by love. This love is to be demonstrated just as Jesus demonstrated His love toward us (Rom. 5:8). In other words, this *agapé* love is unconditional, sacrificial, and exists regardless of changing circumstances. A dedicated faithful love chooses to be given, even when less is received. Jesus said, "A new command I give you: Love one another. As I have loved you, so you must love one another. By this all men will know that you are my disciples, if you love one another" (John 13:34-35). Jesus demonstrated love for the disciples during His earthly ministry. He walked with them. He lived among them. He taught them. He would further display His love on the cross and die for them. Even when the disciples' belief in Jesus wavered, He loved them unconditionally. Additionally, He urged the disciples to love one

another (John 13:1, 15:9, 13; 1 John 3:16). This love would be evidence to an onlooking world that they were His disciples. It was a love that was free, consistent, lavish, and persevering. God is the Author of love. God is love, and Jesus is our example of love.

6. A Disciple Is a Friend of God (vv. 14-15). Jesus said that when we do what He commands, we are no longer servants, but instead, He calls us friends. Abraham and Moses were both referenced as being friends of God (Ja. 2:23; Ex. 33:11). As a result, both of them had intimate encounters with God that enabled them to know God in a deeper way. Being a friend of God opens the door to an immeasurable relationship with Him.

7. A Disciple is Chosen by God (v. 16). Jesus tells us that we did not choose Him, but He chose us. The disciple's relationship with Jesus occurs when the disciple responds to Jesus' bidding. Jesus initiates an invitation to come follow Him, and the disciple responds by leaving everything to pursue of life of obedience to Christ.

As we consider these characteristics, we understand that disciples of Jesus are not merely people who have followed Jesus around to learn from Him, but they are followers who have entered into a new life that causes radical transformation.

▶ The Acts of the Apostles: From Discipleship to Apostleship

The discipling relationship that Jesus displayed with the disciples in the Gospels serves as an example for the discipling relationships for the believers in Acts, as well as for believers today. The apostles and the community of disciples relied on what Jesus had taught them and demonstrated before them, and then, within the context of community and with the power of the Holy Spirit, they emulated what they had witnessed. In Acts, the call of discipleship is also a call for community. The word *disciple* transitions in Acts—from the twelve, as seen in the Gospels; to all believers (Acts 2:44; 4:32; 5:14); to the church after Pentecost (Acts 5:11); and later to all Christians (Acts 11:26).[25] In Acts, the twelve disciples are now referred to as "apostles" as they evolve into leaders of the new community (Acts 1:2, 26; 2:37; 14:4, 14; 15:2, 6).

The book of Acts records that soon after Pentecost, the early church supernaturally expanded to include over three thousand people. During this time, the Grecian Jews complained to the Hebraic Jews because their widows were being overlooked in the daily administration. The apostles gathered the church, and the believers selected seven men who were "known to be full of the Spirit and wisdom" (Acts 6:3). These selected men were given the responsibility to minister to the flock so that the apostles could give their attention to prayer and the ministry of the Word (Acts 6:1-6). This structure of dividing the people enabled the apostles to give full attention to their work as ministers, and the needs of the people were met. Positive results came almost immediately as a result of the wise and effective handling of the Grecians' complaint. The Word of God spread, the gospel continued to bear fruit, and the number of disciples in Jerusalem increased rapidly. The writer Luke, also shows that in spite of opposition from outside of the church and problems within, the gospel was able to continue its remarkable progress.[26] When the responsibility of the daily administration of the local church was shared, the Word of God spread, the number of disciples rapidly increased, and many priests became obedient to the faith (Acts 6:7).

Summary

Although viewing discipleship through the lens of the Old Testament is rarely examined, it is clearly evident. We see that the concept of discipleship plainly began in the Old Testament through biblical covenant relationships, tribal communities, in the Greco-Roman World, in the Hellenistic Era, and within Judaism. The New Testament brings Jesus on the scene, who not only lays the foundation for the process of discipleship, but also demonstrates what it means to be a disciple. He provides a portrait of what a disciple looks like. As we consider discipleship, we must approach it holistically, understanding that God's way of growing the church by means of discipling believers is interwoven throughout the entire Bible.

QUESTIONS TO PONDER

1) Before reading this chapter, had you ever considered the concept of discipleship being present in the Old Testament? What does Jesus' earthly ministry teach you about discipleship?

2) How has your theological understanding of biblical discipleship changed after reading this chapter?

---

[3]Michael Wilkins, *Discipleship in the Ancient World and Matthew's Gospel* (Grand Rapids: Baker Books, 1995), 51.

[4]Examples include the Noahic Covenant (Gen. 6:18, 8:20, 9:9-17); the Abrahamic Covenants (Gen. 12:1-7, 15:9-21, 17:1-21); the Mosaic Covenant (Exod. 19-24); and the Davidic Covenant (2 Sam. 7:4-16). Jonathan Lunde, *Following Jesus, the Servant King: A Biblical Theology of Covenantal Discipleship* (Grand Rapids: Zondervan, 2010), 45-46.

[5]Michael Wilkins, *Following the Master: A Biblical Theology of Discipleship* (Grand Rapids: Zondervan, 1991), 57-58.

[6]Ibid., 59-60.

[7]Ibid., 60-61.

[8]Ibid., 62-63.

[9]Candace Barron, "Small Group Theology: Part One," October 31, 2013, The Network for Discipleship and Mission, United Methodists of Arkansas, accessed October 9, 2014, http://network.arumc.org/spiritual-formation/small-group-theology-part-1, 3.

[10]Bill Hull, *The Complete Book of Discipleship: On Being and Making Followers of Christ* (Colorado Springs: NavPress, 2006), 53.

---

[11]Wilkins, *Following*, 72-75.

[12]Paul R. Spickard and Kevin M. Cragg, *A Global History of Christians: How Everyday Believers Experienced Their World* (Grand Rapids: Baker Academic, 1994), 22.

[13]Wilkins, *Following*, 76.

[14]Wilkins, *Following*, 82-84.

[15]Wilkins, *Following*, 84-86.

[16]Wilkins, *Following*, 84.

[17]Wilkins, *Following*, 86-88.

[18]Wilkins, *Following*, 88.

[19]Barry D. Smith, "Summary of Dead Sea Scrolls," section 3, Crandall University Professor Pages, accessed September 10, 2014, http://www.mycrandall.ca/courses/NTIntro/InTest/Qumran.htm#Q3.

[20]Wilkins, *Following*, 90.

[21]Wilkins, *Following*, 176-83.

[22]H. D. M. Spence and Joseph S. Exell, *The Pulpit Commentary* (1919; repr., Peabody, Mass.: Hendrickson, 1985), 644.

[23]Kenneth S. Wuest, "Mk 10:42," *Wuest's Word Studies from the Greek New Testament: For the English Reader* (Grand Rapids: Eerdmans, 1997).

[24]Wilkins, *Following*, 211.

[25]Wilkins, *Following*, 251-59.

[26]Douglas Redford, *The New Testament Church: Acts-Revelation* (Cincinnati: Stand Publishing, 2007), 36.

CHAPTER TWO

We're Coming Up Short:
The Disciple Deficit

The Problem of Non-Discipleship and Non-Discipleship Christianity

DESPITE THE foundation, standard, and commission for discipleship found in the Bible, many churches are facing the tremendous dilemma of non-discipleship—the lack of, inadequate, or minimal existence, of an effective disciple-making process within the church. The problem of non-discipleship exists because while countless churches have a mission, their mission is not Christ's mission—the Great Commission. Too often Christians focus on the salvation message of the cross and omit instructing people to live lives that adhere to Jesus' teaching.

Countless churches are either oblivious to their lack of attention to making disciples, or they make discipleship an optional choice among an array of ministries and programs offered at the church. As a result, real spiritual growth of countless Christians suffers. Bill Hull argues that this negligence has led to "non-discipleship Christianity that leads to plenty of motion, activity, and conferences but no lasting transformation."[27] The idea of non-discipleship Christianity describes individuals that profess Christianity without a commitment or effort to follow His teaching in every area of their lives. As a result, non-discipleship Christianity produces within Christians an attitude that limits grace to conversion, while excluding a Christian lifestyle. People learn to believe that salvation settles the issue—rather than beginning a lifelong journey of following Christ's teachings. Researcher George Barna reports:

> Most born-again adults (95 percent) acknowledge that their church encourages spiritual growth. But only half of the believers we interviewed felt that discipleship is one of the two or three highest ministry priorities of their church; the other half said it is just one of many ministries or programs at their church.[28]

Christians can grow and mature in a corporate setting (Sunday morning worship) without anyone's viewing them as disciples. However, they grow deeper in an environment where discipleship is affirmed and practiced. In other words, believers need more than a sermon on Sunday mornings. They need to be in an environment where they can tangibly learn how to apply what they are taught on Sundays. Discipleship, then, should not be optional in the local church, but rather the foundation that undergirds and guides the church, as well as every ministry within the church.

Unfortunately, numerous churches do not have a comprehensive plan to transform their people into lifelong learners of Jesus Christ. They have plans for the continuous numerical growth of their church, for various ministry and volunteer opportunities, for finances and budgets, but they do not have a plan to spiritually grow their members. The church has placed emphasis on so many things in an effort to draw the masses. We have started ministries, programs, non-profits, initiatives, had concerts, plays, comedians, and invited the "big-name speakers," all in an effort to draw the crowd. Although nothing is necessarily wrong with any of these emphases, it is imperative that church leaders work hard at keeping the main thing, the main thing by being intentional and strategic in developing disciples of Jesus Christ. Numerous churches have excelled at the theology of decision-making (accepting Christ) but have grossly failed to develop an appropriate strategy for disciple-making. We have struggled to find ways to help ordinary people get beyond the choosing of particular Christian activities and to learn how to think, act, and be like Jesus in every aspect of their lives.

Implications of Non-Discipleship: A Disciple Deficit

As a result of non-discipleship, the church is experiencing a disciple deficit—an insufficient supply of disciples to infiltrate, impact and transform a casual cultural, sinful world. The disciple deficit has had a devastating impact on every system of society. Currently, the Christian faith makes up one third of the population among all religions. However, it is projected that by 2050 the number of Muslims will nearly equal the number of Christians around the world.[31] These numbers demonstrate Christians have a lot of work to do, and if we are not careful, we may find ourselves losing ground in producing disciples of Jesus Christ.

Additionally, just as discipleship bears fruit in a person's life, so does non-discipleship. When Christians are not being intentionally discipled, they neglect to grow spiritually, and that neglect directly impacts outward behavior. According to Putman, Harrington, and Coleman, the fact that Christians are not being effectively discipled is proven statistically. When it comes to morality and lifestyle issues such as divorce, pornography, racism, domestic violence, and drug and alcohol abuse, for example, there is little difference between the behavior of Christians and that of non-Christians.[32] Dallas Willard states,

> There is an obvious Great Disparity between, on the one hand, the *hope for life expressed in Jesus*—found real in the Bible and in many shining examples from among his followers—and, on the other hand, *the actual day-to-day behavior, inner life, and social presence* of most of those who now profess adherence to him.[33]

Omission of the Great Commission results in church-going Christians who are spiritually shallow, exhibit biblical ignorance, and most often do little to advance Christian ministry. It is apparent that non-discipleship can cause one to remain defeated morally, which has broad ramifications for the individual, as well as those in their sphere of influence and beyond. Non-discipleship affects every area of an individual's life and robs believers of experiencing God's empowering grace and desired victory in their lives.

As we study and apply the Word of God, we increasingly change on the inside, which is reflected on the outside. This transformed life directly impacts a person's social context. Discipleship gives people power beyond themselves to deal with the everyday challenges of life. Therefore, salvation alone is not enough, but believers must also be conformed to the image of Christ, which will positively affect the practical aspects of everyday life. Without the invaluable experience of being discipled, individuals are left alone to contend with the realities of life. Willard summarizes the cost of non-discipleship quite well:

> Non-discipleship costs abiding peace, a life penetrated throughout by love, faith that sees everything in the light of God's overriding governance for good, hopefulness that stands firm in the most discouraging of circumstances, power to do

what is right and withstand the forces of evil. In short, non-discipleship costs you exactly that abundance of life Jesus said he came to bring (John 10:10).[34]

Non-discipleship has lasting implications for believers, the church, the community, and the world.

How Do We Measure Growth?

The Christian church has been the cornerstone of the American culture for centuries. However, we are currently in the midst of a paradigm shift and the context of ministry has changed. While many Christians are not walking away from God, they are leaving the church community and practicing their faith outside of the four walls. Many churches are experiencing stagnation, a lack of church growth, and even membership decline. Twenty-five years ago, we saw churches across the country expanding, building larger sanctuaries, adding multiple worship services, and going to a multi-site format to accommodate their growing congregations. Unfortunately, today many of these same churches now find themselves striving to keep afloat financially. Some have incorporated creative ways to generate revenue, such as making the church site a multipurpose event or business facility. Countless churches have combined their multiple worship services, and some have even found the need to move to rental space and/or sell those large edifices.

Many people propose a plethora of reasons why so many churches are facing these challenges. Some say the problem is the result of people not giving to the church as they once did. Others state that while making church available online had many advantages, it negatively impacted the Sunday morning worship attendance. This issue was even prior to the coronavirus pandemic of 2020, which literally closed the doors of churches across the country. Some speculate that church ministries are not meeting the needs of the people—spiritually, physically and socially. Others have concluded that the children's program of many churches is ineffective, and as a result, they are not drawing families. However, I want to suggest that the problem of the lack of growth in many churches is more than a ministry or programmatic problem. It is more than a virtual church, economic or attendance problem. The deeper problem is that the global church has lost her focus, and as a result, we are losing ground in producing disciples of Jesus Christ.

Additionally, amidst some churches that are experiencing stagnation and decline, others are experiencing growth. However, a true assessment might reveal that the growth is not real. In other words, these churches may be experiencing numerical growth, but the people are not experiencing spiritual transformation. It is possible for a church to grow wider without growing deeper. Robert E. Webber quotes African theologian Dr. Tokunboh Adeyemo, who says that the church "is one mile long, but only one inch deep."[29] I have witnessed this in my own ministry. I saw a church rapidly grow from fewer than 200 members to more than 10,000 in a few short years. The church grew from one Sunday morning worship service to two services, then three, and then to multiple sites. While everyone was rejoicing over the numerical growth we were experiencing, there were many Sundays when I sat with tears running down my face. They were tears filled with mixed emotions. I was happy the pews were being filled; however, I grieved inwardly because although the church was growing numerically, it was becoming full of spiritual babes. We were experiencing rapid growth. We were witnessing new converts, the return of long-lost members, and a number of church transfers; but we were not successfully making disciples.

We had nothing to offer the newcomers except New Member Orientation, Sunday school, Mission (the Baptist people know what that is all about), and Brotherhood. While that may sound great, it was not enough. We did not have a structured discipleship ministry as a part of our assimilation process to help these believers grow in their relationship with the Lord, nor did we have a Spiritual Growth Path (to be discussed in Chapter 8) to guide them in their spiritual growth journey. Several years later, the Lord opened the door for me to implement a discipleship strategy, which revolutionized the church. The strategy was nothing phenomenal to my credit. We simply got on board with what Jesus instructed us to do. Henry Blackaby says, "We should look for where God is working and then join him in his work."[30] This was the beginning of a fire being ignited within me to further help churches effectively disciple their people.

So, the problem of non-discipleship is real, and the means by which we measure growth warrants consideration. As a result, we cannot turn our heads to the implications of non-discipleship.

Summary

The answer to the problem of non-discipleship, non-discipleship Christianity, and the disciple deficit is to return to what we have been commissioned to do. Jesus made it clear that believers are to make disciples and not merely converts to Christianity. Discipleship can be experienced only when one comes to understand that salvation marks the beginning of a lifelong commitment of obedience to Christ in every area of your life, every day of your life. Christianity is more than just belief in a set of religious facts. Believing in Jesus without following His teaching has no merit. When Jesus said, "Follow me," He was calling for a decision. True Christianity is not just about salvation but also involves long-term obedience. Additionally, discipleship involves choosing a Christian life that involves both attitude and action, conversion and commitment, salvation, and sanctification because "Faith without works is dead" (James 2:17). Conversion pivots around the cross *and* obedience. It involves salvation from hell in the future and a life committed to the teachings of Jesus in the present. Discipleship is the method Jesus used to expand the kingdom of God, and it is just as effective today.

There is no doubt that there is much disparity between Christians who profess faith in Jesus Christ and the amount of influence they have on the spiritual climate of today. Is it possible that the church has lost momentum and direction? Have we reduced Christianity to only acknowledging Jesus as Savior, while omitting the implications of following Him as Lord? Have we lost our way? My response to these questions is "Yes, but I believe there is hope." I do not believe it is too late. God has always kept a remnant for Himself, and discipleship is no different. By the mere fact that you are reading this book demonstrates that God continues to raise up men and women who desire to return to the Great Commission of making, maturing, multiplying and mobilizing disciples of Jesus Christ to impact the world.

QUESTIONS TO PONDER

1) What other implications of non-discipleship do you see impacting our world today?

2) What are some criteria you, or your church, use to measure growth? Would you say you are measuring what matters most?

[27]Bill Hull, Jesus Christ, *Disciplemaker* (Grand Rapids: Baker, 2004), 10.

[28]George Barna, *Growing True Disciples: New Strategies for Producing Genuine Followers of Christ* (Colorado Springs: Waterbrook Press, 2001), 46.

[29]Robert E. Webber, *Ancient-Future Evangelism: Making You Church a Faith-Forming Community* (Grand Rapids: Baker Books, 2003), 13.

[30]Henry T. Blackaby, Richard Blackaby, and Claude V. King, *Experiencing God: Knowing and Doing the Will of God* (Nashville: Life Way Press, 1990).

[31]Katherine Richey, "Number of Muslims Worldwide Expected to Nearly Equal Number of Christians by 2050; Religiously Unaffiliated Will Make Up Declining Share of World's Population," *Pew Forum*, 2015, accessed August 25, 2019, https://www.pewforum.org/2015/04/02/number-of-muslims-worldwide-expected-to-nearly-equal-number-of-christians-by-2050-religiously-unaffiliated-will-make-up-declining-share-of-worlds-population/.

[32]Jim Putman, Bobby Harrington, and Robert E. Coleman, *Disciple Shift: Five Steps That Help Your Church Make Disciples That Make Disciples* (Grand Rapids: Zondervan, 2013), 20.

[33]Dallas Willard, *The Great Omission* (New York: Harper Collins, 2006), x.

[34]Ibid., 9.

CHAPTER THREE

There Is Hope:
Steps to Address the Problem

A Call to Action

W HILE THE previous chapter established that the problem of non-discipleship and non-discipleship Christianity has resulted in a disciple deficit, this chapter examines some of the fundamental steps church leaders can take to address the problem. They are as follows:

- Prioritize evangelism and discipleship.
- Create a discipleship strategy.
- Encourage believers to have spiritual goals.
- Monitor church calendars for overtaxing activities.
- Require personal discipleship among pastoral leadership.
- Identify a key person to give leadership to the area of discipleship.
- Make discipleship an expectation for membership.
- Ensure all ministry efforts support the commitment to discipleship.

- Increase the discipleship focus in ministry training.
- Facilitate life-transforming relationships through small group discipleship.

Prioritize Evangelism and Discipleship

Some churches place greater emphasis on evangelism, while giving little attention to discipleship. They focus on evangelism at the expense of discipleship by seeking to win converts and not make disciples. However, if church leaders are going to be successful in making disciples, evangelism and discipleship must both be a priority. The Great Commission is two-fold and encompasses baptizing them *and* teaching them. Neither is optional. They exist in a cyclical relationship. Evangelism flows out of discipleship and vice versa. Making converts to Christ and making disciples of Christ are not the same. We must resist the temptation to focus solely on evangelism (winning lost souls) while neglecting discipleship (teaching believers how to live the Christian life until they also are fulfilling the Great Commission). A disservice is done to believers when we lead them to Christ without investing in their spiritual growth and development. As seen with Jesus and His disciples, the commitment to teach involves giving instruction according to the whole counsel of God's Word, so that followers of Jesus Christ might learn to live a life in obedience to His Word, and in turn, reach others with the message of the gospel (Matt 5:2; Mark 11:17).

As we compare the present state of evangelism with that of the New Testament, evangelism methods today provide little to no opportunity to develop relationships. Most often evangelism focuses on decision making rather than disciple making. Evangelistic methods have become so simplistic that they do not adequately prepare believers for how to respond to the needs of non-Christians, as it relates to their day-to-day lives in Christ. It is all about the instantaneous decision to accept Christ in the moment. Evangelism in the New Testament was designed to make disciples. New Testament believers presented the whole gospel and its implications. Making disciples meant reaching non-Christians, teaching them how to grow, and in turn, how to make new disciples. Within the early church, there was no distinction between evangelism, discipleship, and spiritual formation.[35]

Placing more attention on evangelism while giving little attention to discipleship can create a revolving-door syndrome, which involves the influx of new converts coming in the front door of the church in the midst of a mass exodus out the back door. As people are being compelled through the front door, others have become discontented and have moved on to the church down the street. We can become so focused on reaching people that we lose sight of keeping them. Unless we become intentional in closing the back door, it will continue to swing open. This is important because if people do not stay, they cannot be taught, and if they are not taught, they cannot grow into committed, authentic followers of Jesus. Rather than focusing on programs and events to bring people in the front door, churches should focus on serving people well to not only encourage them to stay, but to bring their friends. This presents an organic way to evangelize and disciple.

Create a Discipleship Strategy

In order to address the discipleship deficit, churches must have a discipleship strategy. This does not mean that discipleship is about funneling people through a systematic program, but churches should be intentional in discipling people and have a strategy with goals and objectives in helping their people grow in every area of their lives. Most pastors desire to make disciples and fulfill the Great Commission but are uncertain how to do it.

There are three fundamental non-negotiables for creating an

effective discipleship environment. First, the pastor and church leadership must have a deep conviction about discipleship being taught and modeled. Second, there needs to be a defined vision, purpose, and mission. A church's vision gives direction to its people, and it increases interest, commitment, productivity, and unity. The vision, purpose, and mission should include clear objectives and a plan of action for disciple-making. Third, there needs to be a specific model or intentional strategy. This strategy should be clearly communicated, uncomplicated, easily accessible, and measurable, so that individuals may be challenged to embark upon the pathway to spiritual transformation. A Spiritual Growth Path will be discussed in Chapter 8 to help you develop a disciple-making strategy for your church.

Encourage Believers to Have Spiritual Goals

Not only is it important to have a discipleship strategy, but church members should be encouraged to set spiritual goals. Most people would agree that setting goals is the first step to success in any area. This theory can also apply to spiritual growth and development. However, not all Christians are conscientious about setting goals for their spiritual development, and some fail at setting standards to measure their growth. This creates a great opportunity for churches to help people develop a specific path to foster spiritual growth. Church leaders can help believers identify spiritual goals, along with a strategic process to guide them in their spiritual journeys. This helps to create a culture where the church sets a standard and expectation for the spiritual growth of their members. Helping believers identify spiritual goals, along with a strategic process to guide them, increases the probability of their spiritual growth. This will be further discussed in Chapter 5.

Monitor Church Calendars for Overtaxing Activities

Many churches are overtaxed by prioritizing a variety of issues, such as Sunday worship attendance, finances, meetings, building construction, activities, programs, and events. While nothing is wrong with these activities and the business side of ministry should not be neglected, churches can become complicated and over-programmed. Overtaxing members in an array of activities that give little attention to making disciples of Jesus Christ is easy. If we are not careful, the busyness of ministry can lead to producing people who focus on *doing* rather than *being*. Additionally, it is not uncommon for pastors and ministry leaders to suffer from over-functioning. Most of us who are called into ministry also carry a passion for it. As a result, if we are not mindful, we can find ourselves doing more than what is necessary or required.

The dysfunction of an over-functioning leader can create an over-functioning church. This busyness can literally exhaust church staff and members, yet they may feel obligated or less spiritual if they are not involved, present, and available every time the church door opens. Leaders can avoid this rat race when they minimize the complexity that encourages busyness without effectiveness. Ministry focus should be simple and designed to help fulfill the mission and purpose of the church, rather than to arbitrarily be engaged in meaningless busywork. Church leaders must reassess the nature, purpose, quantity, and quality of activities they implement within their churches and determine how those activities are supporting or impeding the spiritual development of their members.

It is vital that church leaders weed out the clutter and ask themselves the right questions.

- ► Is our time, focus, and resources going toward our priorities as stated in our vision and mission statement?

- ► Are souls being saved?

► Are the needs of our families being met?

► Are we making a difference in our community and world?

► Are lives being transformed?

► Are we making disciples?

These are the questions that matter. The standards of secular success of buildings, bodies, and bucks can cause us to settle for artificial stimulation rather than real spiritual power. We must ensure that we do not become preoccupied with structural issues at the expense of spiritual vitality.

Require Personal Discipleship among Pastoral Leadership

It is possible for pastors to preach, teach, lead, serve, and encourage others in their spiritual development, while neglecting their own. Many pastors do not give serious attention to their own personal spiritual formation, and as a result, they do not model discipleship among their members. It is important for the pastor to be the forerunner in the area of discipleship. Senior leadership needs to cheerlead the discipleship process. Teaching and preaching about discipleship and sharing stories about their personal spiritual growth motivates and encourages church members to also engage in discipleship. It helps make discipleship a part of the culture of the church. It is difficult for leaders to guide others to a place they have not been, nor are willing to go. Humble leaders subject themselves to the guidance and instruction of others, and they are accountable to others. They allow others to speak into their lives and provide godly counsel and constructive feedback from which they can develop and grow. Wise leaders subject themselves to what they teach, and they lead by example.

It can be more challenging to engage the majority of the church in the process of discipleship when the pastor does not wholeheartedly take ownership and embrace the goal to be discipled and to disciple church members. Pastors and church leaders cannot merely visualize or talk about discipleship, but they must do it. Only when church leaders are sincere about their own discipleship to Jesus can churches make discipleship a priority where authentic disciples are being produced and reproduced. People are more likely to engage in discipleship, grow spiritually, and become disciple-makers when their leaders are doing the same.

Identify a Key Person to Give Leadership to the Area of Discipleship

Having a key person or team to lead the discipleship ministry of the church is imperative. This person(s) could be a staff member, volunteer, or a team consisting of both. Though the title is not as important as the function, this person could be referred to as the Discipleship Pastor, Minister of Discipleship, Discipleship Leader, Discipleship Coach, Small Group Minister, Family Pastor, etc. This person serves to ensure that the mission of discipleship is effectively and consistently carried out throughout the church. He/she should be trained in the area of discipleship and should understand the biblical mandate for making disciples. They should have a love, vision, and passion for making disciples. They should also have the ability to lead, plan, coordinate and implement the church's discipleship ministry. Additionally, he or she should have the capability to work well with people and train others, as in keeping with Jesus' discipleship model.

Make Discipleship an Expectation for Membership

Many churches follow a "membership" model rather than a "discipleship" model. Following the membership model enables people to become church members without the expectation of becoming committed followers of Jesus Christ. The membership model cultivates an environment that is conducive for non-growing, non-fruit-bearing disciples. People become content with simply being members. Most often they are not challenged to engage in discipleship, and little expectation or accountability is placed upon them to prioritize their spiritual growth. Consequently, they may not see the relevance of the Word of God in their lives and hence live in contrast to Jesus' teaching.

Churches that settle for the membership model do not create an environment that fosters strong, spiritually maturing believers. This can lead to a church where only a few people do all of the work, which is often the pastor or established leaders. Additionally, members often become complacent and comfortable sitting in the pews being entertained rather than actively engaging in ministry. Because only a few people are doing the work of ministry, newcomers will either leave because they do not feel welcomed, needed, and included, or they will come in and get comfortable on the pew. Addressing the discipleship deficit involves churches adopting the discipleship model, which places an expectation on every member who confesses Jesus as Lord to embark upon the journey of discipleship, spiritual growth and service.

Ensure All Ministry Efforts Support the Commitment to Discipleship

It is possible for church leaders to believe they are making disciples when indeed, they are not. In addition to Sunday morning worship service, most churches offer Bible studies and Sunday school. It can be assumed that because congregants are attending these various activities, they are producing growing and thriving followers of Jesus. Often, these well-intended efforts are not enough. Sunday worship, Sunday school, and even Bible studies are not necessarily discipleship.

Discipleship is more than offering a class and more than listening to a Bible study lesson or sermon. Discipleship involves helping people to embark upon a life-transforming, ongoing, progressive path of spiritual growth with others who are on the same journey. Discipleship is a more comprehensive approach than simply attending church on Sunday or a class through the week. It involves a necessary relational aspect, where people engage in the Word together and have opportunity to do life together. Pastors and church leaders must assess whether their ministry efforts are not just providing people with information, but rather creating an environment for transformation.

Increase the Discipleship Focus in Ministry Training

The academy must play a part in closing the gap of the discipleship deficit. It is vitally important that pastors and church leaders be adequately trained for contextualized discipleship. If making disciples is indeed the mission of the church, as established by Matthew 28:19-20, then seminaries and Bible colleges bear a responsibility to equip ministry leaders for this area of ministry. It is imperative that schools offer strong curriculums—not just for youth ministry, children's ministry, preaching, evangelism, church administration, Christian education, and the like; but there must be a comprehensive curriculum to prepare those who are entering ministry to prioritize discipleship. They must be equipped with the understanding of biblical discipleship and have the practical tools to implement it within their ministry settings. Many believe that discipleship is a specific area of ministry. However, because discipleship is the foundation that undergirds every area of ministry, discipleship training should be included as a part of educating Christians.

Facilitate Life-transforming Relationships through Small Group Discipleship

Having a discipleship infrastructure within your church fosters an easy and accessible process for individuals to join a small group and connect with people who are also on a spiritual journey. Small groups provide a means for intentional, effective, and impactful relationships to develop among people. They create an environment conducive for spiritual development and connection. Chapter 4 will discuss in more detail the significance for small group discipleship, and Chapter 9 will provide practical steps on implementing small groups within your church.

Additional Solutions for Filling the Discipleship Gap

As we have examined some fundamental steps church leaders can take to address the problem of non-discipleship, Greg Ogden also addresses this issue as he describes seven marks of discipleship that, if exercised, will fill the gap between the biblical standard and the reality in the Christian community.[36] He concludes that if addressed, these marks of discipleship can fill the discipleship deficit.

1. *Proactive Ministers versus Passive Recipients.*[37] Many believers come to the church as spectators. They worship but do not see themselves as active ministers. Church leaders must teach people that they are not passive recipients in the pews; rather, these leaders must develop and deploy their congregants as proactive ministers. Ogden writes, "The New Testament picture of the church is an every-member ministry. The 'priesthood of all believers' is not just a Reformation watchword but also a radical biblical ideal."[38]

2. *Spiritually Undisciplined versus Spiritually Disciplined.*[39] Followers of Jesus are identified by a disciplined way of life. The Bible often likens the Christian journey to a race (1 Tim. 4:7-8; Gal. 5:7, Heb. 12:1, Jas. 1:12). The Christian life is a race to be contrasted by a marathon versus a sprint. The race requires discipline, long-term obedience, and endurance. Church leaders must model and teach a lifetime and lifestyle of discipline and obedience to God's Word.

3. *Holistic Discipleship versus Private Faith.*[40] Discipleship should impact every area of a person's life, and its results should be able to be witnessed by others. The demonstration of a person's faith should not be divided into a public versus private realm or secular versus spiritual. Christians must understand that everything is spiritual, and the life of an authentic disciple is integrated and congruent.

4. *Countercultural Force versus Blending In.*[41] Ogden writes, "The church in the biblical scheme is a body whose collective lifestyle forms a countercultural alternative to the values of the dominant society."[42] The Christian community is to be a countercultural force not conforming to the dominant society. Believers are called to operate in this world but not of the world (John 17:16).

5. *Essential Church versus Church is optional.*[43] Scriptures describe the church as an essential, living organism through which the incarnate Jesus continues to manifest Himself through His people. Thus, the church is necessary. The church is a community, and people are discipled within community; therefore, the church is essential to every believer.

6. *Biblically Informed versus Biblically Illiterate people.*[44] Ogden writes, "Scriptures picture believers as biblically informed people whose lives are founded on revealed truth."[45] If Christians are going to make an impact on the spiritual climate in today's world, we must be biblically informed and transformed. This necessitates teaching the whole counsel of the Bible with accuracy. Discipleship helps prevent biblically illiterate Christians.

7. *People Who Share Their Faith versus People Who Do Not Share Their Faith.*[46] Disciples of Jesus Christ are depicted by their willingness to share the story of their faith, and as a result, further perpetuate the message of the gospel. Discipling individuals can teach and give them confidence to share the Gospel.

Observing these seven marks of discipleship can help close the gap between the biblical standard for Christianity and the reality of the disciple deficit we are experiencing in the world.

Summary

This chapter has provided a few ways churches can begin to address the problem of non-discipleship within their church. Tackling the disciple deficit that has resulted in society will require church leaders to make an honest assessment of how their church is doing in the specific areas discussed and then be willing to take the necessary steps for change. When a person breaks a bone, it requires resetting in order for healing to occur. Addressing the problem of non-discipleship and filling in the gap between the biblical standard and the reality of the spiritual condition of most Christians will require some churches to reset their past practices and priorities.

QUESTIONS TO PONDER

1) How have you, or how has your church addressed the problem of non-discipleship and non-discipleship Christianity? What grade would you give yourself or your church for addressing this dilemma?

2) In addition to the solutions discussed in this chapter, what other ways might you address the problem of non-discipleship and non-discipleship Christianity?

---

[35]Webber, *Ancient-Future Evangelism,* 20-25.

[36]Greg Ogden, *Transforming Discipleship: Making Disciples a Few at a Time* (Downers Grove, Ill.: InterVarsity, 2003), 24-25.

[37]Ibid., 24.

[38]Ibid.

[39]Ibid., 25-27.

[40]Ibid., 27-29.

[41]Ibid., 29-31.

[42]Ibid., 30.

[43]Ibid., 31-33.

[44]Ibid., 33-35.

[45]Ibid., 33.

[46]Ibid., 35-37.

CHAPTER FOUR

Connecting the Dots:
Small Group Discipleship

Discipleship and Small Groups

ISCIPLESHIP IS an ongoing process of becoming more and more like Jesus (transformation) through learning and obeying His Word. This happens most effectively within the context of relationships with others who are on the same journey. Discipleship should not be viewed as a mere program or a specific curriculum on a checklist of an array of other ministry offerings. Rather, discipleship is an intentional process put in place for the purpose of lives being transformed into the image of Christ.

Small groups have proven to be an effective strategy that promotes spiritual growth. When successfully implemented, small groups can promote authentic disciples as they learn the Word of God and learn how to apply it to their daily lives. For the purpose of this book, a small group is defined as an assembly of three to twelve people who are engaged in discipleship together through intentional gatherings. Together, they share the goal of personal, spiritual, and emotional formation through the study of God's Word, Christian edification, and fellowship. Small groups intentionally and strategically provide an environment for connection and community.

Small Group Discipleship in the Early Church

As addressed in chapter one, discipleship is present in the Old and New Testaments. Additionally, small group discipleship can be substantiated throughout the history of the early church. House churches, a part of the early church culture, was necessary due to Christians being persecuted. As the apostle Paul began his missionary journeys throughout the Mediterranean, many of the churches he established assembled in various homes. Christian communities came into existence and multiplied. Many of these communities or churches were small gatherings to which Paul was committed.

Paul's final words to the church in Corinth included greetings from Aquila and Priscilla, along with the church that met in their house (1 Cor. 16:19). Reference is also made of the historical event in which Peter went to the home of Cornelius and preached to the Gentiles; while he preached, the Holy Spirit fell upon those present (Acts 10:24-48), making salvation possible for both the circumcised and the uncircumcised—the Jews and the Gentiles (Acts 11:18). Paul refers to the "whole Church" (Rom. 16:23; 1 Cor. 14:23), which implies to me that small groups existed.

The six biblical purposes of the church that were foundational to the early church are found in Acts 2:42-47. These purposes include the following:

1) Teaching of the Word: "they devoted themselves to the apostles' teaching"

2) Fellowship: "and to the fellowship, to the breaking of bread"

3) Prayer: "and to prayer"

4) Unity and ministering to one another: "all the believers were together and had everything in common...they gave to anyone as he had need"

5) Worship: "every day they continued to meet together in the temple courts"

6) Evangelizing: "and the Lord added to their number daily those who were being saved."

The small group discipleship model was the foundation of the early Church and continues to provide a solid foundation for the Church today.

Small Groups of Yesterday and Today

Boren lists five contrasts between the focus of small groups of today and that of small groups during the 1950s, 1960s, and 1970s. First, small groups of the past were more kingdom-focused. Boren believes that unlike many small groups today, small groups in the past did not focus on church growth, the number of groups, or other statistical issues, but rather considered small groups as a means of accomplishing God's greater mission. They were kingdom focused.[47] He writes, "They had a vision for the redemption of creation and for empowering people to have a role in this redemption."[48] Second, small group members of the past lived as kingdom citizens. Boren continues,

> They were looking for the kind of life that reflected the kingdom of God as represented by Jesus. They were not just study groups that met once per week or twice per month. They were groups that knew they had a call to be salt and light in the midst of the world.[49]

Third, small groups of the past did not "water down" the vision.[50] They were not afraid to set boundaries, speak the truth of God's Word, and stand for what was right. Boren writes, "These prophets were not afraid to 'draw the line in the sand' and release those who would not enter the radical call to missional life."[51] Fourth, small groups of the past implemented training consistently. They understood that if the church was to be radically different, extensive training was necessary. Fifth, small groups of the past were open to a new way. Rather than stagnating with a particular model, structure, or curriculum, they used small groups "to experiment with different ideas of being God's people out in front of a watching world."[52]

In essence, we might conclude that according to Boren, many of the issues that we see today with non-discipleship, non-discipleship Christianity, and the disciple deficit were not as prevalent as they are today. However, as we seek to address these issues, small group discipleship continues to be an effective method in making disciples of Jesus Christ; helping Christians to grow spiritually, gain a sense of community, and participate in the mission of God.

The Benefits of Small Groups

A church that follows a biblical discipleship model will not merely offer small groups as an option among many ministries but will be a church that is built with small groups. While discipleship can effectively occur through various methods, there are advantages to using small groups. Small groups can create a caring, supportive environment that cannot be experienced during Sunday morning worship service because of the larger number of people and inability to engage on a personal level. Small groups create an environment that includes trust, grace, humility, encouragement, and affirmation. They create a community where people can flourish and grow. Within the context of small group discipleship individuals live life together, wrestle with and find biblical answers for life's challenges, ask questions, and come to learn the practical elements of God's Word.

Small group discipleship is an effective means of fostering spiritual formation. This can be attributed to the following factors:

1. Small groups are biblical and are instrumental in transforming the lives of God's people to reflect Him.

2. Small groups provide an atmosphere for spiritual growth. They foster an environment where people can become vulnerable before God and their group members.

3. Small groups help individuals learn the Word of God as well as the principles of God's Word. As a result, believers learn to apply God's principles to every area of their lives.

4. Small groups are convenient and flexible and are usually not under the time constraints of the Sunday morning worship service. Groups can meet almost anywhere and at any time, making it conducive for conversation and intimacy. This can also be less taxing on church staff to have to be at the church at varying times to provide access to the building.

5. Small groups help foster and nurture relationships that perhaps would not ordinarily take place. Without them it is easy for church members to get lost in the crowd.

6. Small groups foster accountability. Within the context of transparent relationships, group members can hold one another accountable in areas of struggle and difficulty.

7. Small groups bring encouragement and strength to individuals through the ability to pray for one another and walk alongside each other when life's problems and adversity arise.

8. Small groups are excellent for training. They provide an opportunity for spiritual gifts to be discovered and utilized. As a result, they can be a vehicle to recruit, train, and sustain volunteers.

9. Small groups can be utilized as a leadership pipeline. Many churches are on the decline because new leaders are not being devel-

oped, and their current leaders are getting older and are often burned out. Small groups can provide a place where leaders are continuously being discovered, developed, and deployed.

10.   Small groups are a tool for evangelism. They are an excellent training ground and a vehicle for reproduction. As believers are being discipled, they are growing in their relationship with Jesus. As a result, they are being trained to share their faith and learn to disciple others. Their personal transformation becomes their witness to share with others. Additionally, many people may be willing to attend a small group but unwilling to attend church. Small groups provide a less threatening atmosphere for many people. "Some want to *belong* before they are willing to *believe*."[53]

11.   Small groups help close the back door. Many churches experience the revolving door syndrome because as new people come, they are not being formally discipled and connected. Some people really want to do more than just sit in the pews. Small groups provide a way for them to connect and get involved. When people are connected, they are less likely to leave. Remember, we are called to make disciples—not merely converts.

12.   Small group discipleship produces healthy believers, and healthy believers create healthy families, healthy communities, healthy churches and a healthy world.

13.   Small groups can become an extension of the pastor's hands. They reduce the span of care ratio and can support church leadership with pastoral care, thus taking the load off of the senior pastor for having sole responsibility for the needs of the people.

14.   Small groups help individuals identify their spiritual gifts and begin to utilize them within and without the church.

Pastoral Concerns with Small Groups

Some pastors stand adamantly against small groups. Usually there are two main reasons for this concern. First, some pastors believe that small groups can become social clubs and get messy. While this scenario is indeed a possibility, it reveals the importance of small group facilitators being spiritually mature and adequately trained in leading small groups. There must be specific criteria and clear guidelines in place for small group facilitators (see Chapter 8). Second, many pastors are concerned that small groups open the door for overly zealous group facilitators to take advantage of their influence and initiate division within the church. This disruption can cause churches to split. Again, this issue goes back to the importance of appointing spiritually mature leaders who have demonstrated their commitment as a disciple to Jesus Christ.

The argument against small group discipleship fails to compare to the advantages of having them. When effective training and support is provided to church leadership, internal capacity is built. As a result, the great benefits of the biblical model of small group discipleship is experienced.

Summary

Small group discipleship is not a new phenomenon. The concept of discipleship is found in the Old Testament, and small group discipleship is modeled in the New Testament with Jesus and the disciples. It was evident in the early church. Somehow with time, this effective method of making disciples of Jesus Christ has been lost. Willard states, "So far as the visible Christian institutions of our day are concerned, *discipleship clearly is optional*." Maybe the church does not need to search for new ideas for maturing believers in the faith. We need only look at the foundation that has already been laid. Manskar states the following:

Church leaders are looking for programs and techniques that will help them invite people into a relationship with Jesus Christ, form them as disciples and send them into the world to serve and live the gospel. The tendency, however, is to look for all things "new." All the while our spiritual ancestors have much to offer, especially with regard to small groups as places of faith formation, learning, and transformation.[55]

Perhaps when it comes to small group discipleship, church leaders of today can learn a great deal from church leaders of the past.

The following chapters will discuss three main outcomes of small group discipleship, which include: spiritual growth, a sense of community, and participation in the mission of God.

QUESTIONS TO PONDER

1) Have you ever participated in a discipleship small group? What did you find most helpful? What challenges did you or your group face?

2) What are some additional benefits of small group discipleship? How can church leaders and participants ensure that small groups are healthy and fruitful?

[47]Boren, *Missiorelate*, 30.

[48]Boren, *Missiorelate*, 31.

[49]Boren, *Missiorelate*.

[50]Boren, *Missiorelate*.

[51]Boren, *Missiorelate*.

[52]Boren, *Missiorelate*.

[53]Andy Stanley and Bill Willits, *Creating Community: 5 Keys to Building a Small Group Culture* (Colorado Springs: Multnomah Books, 2004), 95.

[54]Willard, *Omission*, 4.

[55]Manskar, *Accountability*, 3.

Be Ye Transformed:
Spiritual Growth and Spiritual Growth Outcomes

Defining Spiritual Growth

I DEFINE SPIRITUAL growth as the continual transformation that takes place when Christians yield their heart, mind, will, and soul to Jesus Christ. Spiritual growth is reflected in every area of the individual's life (home, community, world, thoughts, behavior, speech, motives, relationships, public life, and private life) and is often evident to others. This does not mean that the individual reaches perfection, but that he is being made perfect through Jesus Christ.

Spiritual depth can be enhanced among Christians when the church community upholds a working definition of spiritual growth and has an effective strategy in place to support it. We cannot assume that because people are attending church, programs are being offered, the Bible is being taught, and ministries are available, people are growing spiritually. There must be clear goals with specific objectives in place to guide the process of helping individuals grow. We must assess whether what we are putting forth is in alignment with the Word of God and then make the necessary adjustments to meet those expectations. This means that churches must prioritize two things. First, spiritual growth outcomes must be clearly defined. This involves articulating what it means to be a healthy, spiritually mature follower of Jesus. Second, there must be an avenue of relational engagement and accountability that people maintain.

The Process of Spiritual Growth

Biblical discipleship involves a progression of spiritual development that occurs over a period of time. As Jesus first called the disciples to follow Him, He clearly called them to a life of a progressive relationship with Him (Matt. 4:18-22; Mark 1:16:20; Luke 5:27; John 1:35-51). Jesus did not call them to be mere acquaintances, but to a relationship that would evolve over time both individually and collectively. The disciples came to have an intimate relationship with Jesus which is demonstrated in three stages. In the first stage, they were occasional companions. Early on they were merely believers and their relationship with Jesus was a matter of convenience (John 2:1, 12, 22; 3:22; 4:1-27).

The second stage involved a profession of faith by each disciple and the renouncement of his secular calling (Mark 1:14-20; 2:13-14). They were called to abandon their former lives and commit and surrender to a life committed to following Jesus. The third stage involved growth and training for leadership. They were chosen to be equipped for the great work of apostleship (Matt. 28:19-20; Luke 6:12-16; John 14:12; Acts 1:8).[56] Likewise, our walk with Jesus occurs in stages and is progressive. Peter urges, "Grow in the grace and knowledge of our Lord and Savior Jesus Christ" (2 Pet. 3:18). The writer of Hebrews concurs by writing, "Let us leave the elementary teachings about Christ and go on to maturity, not laying again the foundation of repentance from acts that lead to death, and of faith in God" (Heb. 6:1).

The Bible speaks of growing spiritually, just as it speaks of growing physically. Samuel is said to have grown in "stature and in favor with the Lord and with men" (1 Sam. 2:26); John the Baptist "grew and became strong in spirit" (Luke 1:30), and Jesus "grew and became strong; he was filled with wisdom, and the grace of God was upon him" (Luke 2:40, 52). The apostle Paul states that the diversity of spiritual gifts was given to the church so that believers would no longer be infants but would "in all things grow up into him who is the Head, that is Christ" (Eph. 4:15b). Though our relationship in Christ is absolute, our fellowship with Him is relative. In other words, our position and relationship with Christ is set, but our condition and fellowship involve a process of taking in the truth of God's Word and growing on the basis of believing and responding to that truth. Spiritual growth is an ongoing process and can only be experienced by understanding and acting on the truth of God's Word.

In essence, to grow spiritually, a person must be "built up in the faith" (Col. 2:7), and this is accomplished progressively and intentionally. The apostle Peter writes that Christian graces are experienced in incremental phases:

> For this reason, make every effort to add to your faith goodness; and to goodness, knowledge; and to knowledge, self-control; and to self-control, perseverance; and to perseverance, godliness; and to godliness, brotherly kindness; and to brotherly kindness, love. For if you possess these qualities in increasing measure, they will keep you from being ineffective and unproductive in your knowledge of our Lord Jesus Christ. (2 Pet. 1:5-8)

The phrase "possess these qualities in increasing measure" points to the ongoing, never-finished aspect of the transformation process.

Transformation: The Goal of Discipleship

Through spiritual growth, transformation of the heart takes place. This inner transformation is the goal of discipleship. "A student is not above his teacher, but everyone who is fully trained will be like his teacher" (Luke 6:40; Matt. 10:24-25). It should be the goal of every disciple to be like Jesus. The apostle Paul writes, "My dear children, for whom I am again in pains of childbirth until Christ is formed in you" (Gal. 4:19). While there are varying views on the interpretation of Paul's statement, "Christ be formed in you," most sources agree that Paul was referring to the spiritual development of the believers' inner life, to the extent that it impacted their outward behavior. The verb, "form" (μορφόω) is translated as "mold." It also means "to give shape to, or fashion" (figurative).[57] Paul used the analogy of the severe pain of childbirth, stating his deep desire for the Galatian believers' lives to be shaped and fashioned into the likeness of Jesus. Though it may be difficult to translate the phrase, "until Christ is formed in you," it is apparent that Paul had an intense desire to see them become like Christ. He wanted them to experience life in the Spirit and possess the characteristics of Christ himself.

Inner transformation causes an individual to move beyond mere outward compliance with Jesus' teaching and embrace a life of obedience that comes from the heart. External manifestation is not the goal of discipleship; the goal is an inner change that ignites a life of obedience to the Spirit of God, through the empowering grace of God in Christ. Additionally, transformation does not occur merely by an accumulation of facts and information, through reading or memorizing Scripture. Nor does it happen through striving to act in conformity with the Word of God. Both of these will only create an attempt to be Christlike through human attainment and legalism, such as was seen in the days of the Scribes and Pharisees (Matt. 5:20; Mark 12:38-40).

Transformation occurs when the Word of God is received and obeyed, and then by the grace of God, through a willing heart, the person is changed from the inside out. James writes,

> Do not merely listen to the word, and so deceive yourselves. Do what it says. Anyone who listens to the word but does not do what it says is like a man who looks at his face in a mirror and, after looking at himself, goes away and immediately forgets what he looks like. But the man who looks intently into the perfect law that gives freedom, and continues to do this, not forgetting what he has heard, but doing it—he will be blessed in what he does (James 1:22-25).

James explains that a person who sees the Word of God as information only or as merely a behavior modifier is like a man who leaves a mirror and forgets what he looks like. However, when a person intently studies and obeys the Word, allowing it to set him free and does so continuously, he will witness the transforming power of the Holy Spirit. Clearly the Bible establishes the foundation that the Christian life involves a lifelong commitment to ongoing spiritual growth and obedience.

Spiritual Growth Outcomes

Many Christians will admit that they want to grow spiritually, and many pastors will say they desire for their members to do so. However, very few Christians know how, and very few church leaders have clearly defined spiritual growth outcomes for their people. This can be attributed to two main reasons: First, although people say they want to grow spiritually, they do not have a plan to help them do so. They do not have a personal spiritual growth strategy in place or even understand the need for one. Second, many churches do not have a spiritual growth path outlined for their members to help them achieve specific spiritual growth goals. A spiritual growth path is a strategic plan designed to guide church members in their spiritual development. This process should be clear, concise, and communicated regularly. The foundation of the spiritual growth path must be discipleship-focused and should be the foundation of the church. This is crucial because some Christians do not understand the process of spiritual growth and maturity. Additionally, they have no idea what their church expects from them as it relates to spiritual growth. Oftentimes, church leaders place more emphasis on the expectation for participation in ministries and activities, rather than on the expectation for spiritual growth and development. As a result, churchgoers begin to measure their relationship with God by activity and *doing*, rather than intimacy with Jesus and *being*. Having spiritual growth outcomes provides an enormous opportunity to help people move from spiritual complacency to a deeper relationship with Jesus.

When a person enrolls in a university to get a degree, an academic degree plan is provided. This plan has specific learning objectives to guide the student in the learning process. Over the course of several years, by following the degree plan, specific information is gained by the student that enables him or her to gain proficient knowledge in a specific area, thus maximizing success. The student is not left to figure it out alone. An advisor helps guide the student through the learning process. This process is no different within the church with spiritual growth. Articulating and implementing clear spiritual objectives and a method of measuring the progress is vital to the discipleship process.

This leads us to explore some specific guidelines for spiritual growth outcomes, which should include the following:

- Spiritual outcomes should be **biblical**. They should reflect biblical principles and Jesus' teaching.

- Spiritual outcomes should be **practical**. They should be applicable to an individual's life and useful for personal evaluation.

- Spiritual outcomes should be **teachable**. They should be clearly communicated in a concise, transportable manner, so that people come away with a clear vision and understanding to set personal goals.

- Spiritual outcomes should be **transforming**. If they are indeed biblical, they will be transforming. Lives will be changed as a result.

- Spiritual outcomes should be **measurable**. Members should be able to measure their personal growth through a specific assessment tool.

Glenn McDonald, in his book, *The Disciple-Making Church: From Dry Bones to Spiritual Vitality*, shares that outcomes of spiritual growth should be:

> *biblical* (that is, an accurate reflection of Jesus' own teaching); *simple* (understandable by adults and children alike); *teachable* (easy to grasp and a cinch to memorize); *practical* (useful for a disciple's self-evaluation); *balanced* (respectful of all of the historical schools of Christian thought and practice that have informed us of the richness of what it means to follow Jesus); and *visionary* (able to serve as the benchmark and the curriculum for everything a congregation might attempt to do and to be).[58]

McDonald presents comprehensive yet simple objectives for spiritual growth. He further introduces "The Six Marks of a Disciple," which are spiritual outcomes that he embraces as characteristics of a man or woman who is learning to live like Jesus. These characteristics include

▶ A Heart for Christ Alone

- ▸ A Mind Transformed by the Word

- ▸ Arms of Love

- ▸ Knees for Prayer

- ▸ A Voice to Speak the Good News

- ▸ A Spirit of Servanthood and Stewardship[59]

While there could be many other characteristics, McDonald presents these marks as fundamental to Christian discipleship. Similarly, Steve Gladen provides spiritual growth outcomes through a spiritual health assessment designed to help people evaluate how well they are balancing five biblical purposes.[60] These areas include worship ("You Were Planned for God's Pleasure"), fellowship ("You Were Formed for God's Family"), discipleship ("You Were Created to Become Like Christ"), ministry ("You Were Shaped for Serving God"), and evangelism ("You Were Made for a Mission").[61] Once individuals have completed the assessment, they are able to identify any weak areas and develop an action plan for growth in that area. LifeWay Christian Resources also has a Spiritual Growth Assessment that evaluates six spiritual disciplines, which include 1) abide in Christ, 2) live in the Word, 3) pray in faith, 4) fellowship with believers, 5) witness to the world, and 6) minister to others.[62]

Summary

Discipleship is only successful to the degree to which individuals are growing spiritually, and spiritual growth can only be determined when there are clearly defined outcomes and assessment tools utilized. Churches that are most effective in defining successful discipleship utilize some type of tool to measure spiritual progress in the lives of congregants.[63] It must be noted that inventories do not provide a completely accurate assessment of the reality of spiritual growth. They are not utilized for the purpose of making any valid claims. However, they are implemented as a personalized indicator of year-to-year growth or achievement of specific personal spiritual growth goals.

QUESTIONS TO PONDER

1) What does spiritual growth look like to you?

2) Describe 3-5 spiritual outcomes that you believe embrace characteristics of a person who is learning to live like Jesus.

[56]Alexander Balmain Bruce, *Training the Twelve* (Memphis: General Books, 2009), 9.

[57]William D. Mounce, "μορφόω," *The Analytical Lexicon to the Greek New Testament* (Grand Rapids: Zondervan, 1993), 324.

[58]Glenn McDonald, The Disciple-Making Church: From Dry Bones to Spiritual Vitality (Lima, Ohio: FaithWalk, 2007), 123.

[59]Ibid., 123.

[60]Steve Gladen, *Small Groups with Purpose: How to Create Healthy Communities* (Grand Rapids: Baker Books, 2013), 127-47.

[61]Ibid., 128-31.

[62]LifeWay, "Spiritual Growth Assessment," accessed June 14, 2012, http://www.lifeway.com/lwc/files/lwcF_PDF_DSC_Spiritual_Growth_Assessment.pdf, 3-4.

[63]Barna, *Growing*, 111.

CHAPTER SIX

We Are in This Thing Together:
Creating a Sense of Community

Defining a Sense of Community

I DEFINE a sense of community as the relationship among a group of Christians who view the group as a spiritual family. Their interaction with one another is genuine and authentic, which fosters love, transparency, and accountability, and creates an environment for spiritual transformation. Their relationship is not exempt from conflict and disharmony. However, there is a general sense, even if unspoken, of individual lives being a part of a whole, and they reflect God individually and collectively.

God Exists in Community

The reality of community has always been a part of God's plan. As God exists in community, He created humanity to be in community. Community reflects the reality of God Himself.

The Trinitarian nature of God is one of the basic tenets of the belief system of Christianity. Although the word *Trinity* is not found in the Bible, the Trinitarian nature of God is supported in Scripture (1 Cor. 12:4; 1 Pet. 1:2). The early church fathers believed that God was one substance, *homoousia*.[64] This belief is the foundation for Christianity's being a monotheistic religion. However, they also believed that God exists in three persons, *hypostases*.[65] The Councils of Nicaea (in 325) and Constantinople (in 381) gave words to affirm the early theologians' belief of three members of the triune God: God the Father, Son, and Holy Spirit.[66] Although God's singularity is foundational to the doctrine of the universal church (Deut. 6:4; 32:39; 2 Sam. 7:22; Ps. 86:10; Mark 12:29; Eph. 4:6), God demonstrated His communal nature in creation.

When God created the world, "the Spirit of God was hovering over the waters" (Gen. 1:2). For everything God created in the book of Genesis, He said, "Let there be" (Gen. 1: 3, 6, 14), except for when He created man, about whom He said, "Let *us* make man in *our* image, in *our* likeness" (Gen. 1:26). Genesis 3:22 is similar, stating, "The man has now become like one of us, knowing good and evil." Creation is founded upon the triune reality of God. It is the result of God the Father, God the Son, and God the Holy Spirit, all working together. The Father created the world through the Son, by His Spirit.

Also substantiating the existence of the Trinity throughout the Old Testament is Genesis 11:7, which reads, "Come, let *us* go down and confuse their language so they will not understand each other." Later, God speaks through Isaiah and Isaiah writes, "Who will go for *us*?" (Is. 6:8). The apostle John states, "In the beginning was the Word, and the Word was with God, and the Word was God. He was with God in the beginning" (John 1:1-2). The apostle Paul similarly writes, "Yet for us there is but one God, the Father, from whom all things came and for whom we live; and there is but one Lord, Jesus Christ, through whom all things came and through whom we live" (1 Cor. 8:6). The expression of the Trinity is also found in 2 Corinthians 13:14: "May the grace of the Lord Jesus Christ, and the love of God, and the fellowship of the Holy Spirit be with you all."

Early theologians thoroughly examined these and other Scriptures which led them to establish the doctrine of the Trinity, identifying one God who exists in three persons. God the Father, God the Son, and God the Holy Spirit have always existed as one, yet in community. The Trinity dwells in perfect unity and community. Because God operates in community and because we are made in His image, we too are created in and for community.

Jesus Is Our Example of Living in Community

Jesus' public ministry modeled what it meant to be and live in community. He was in community with the Father. He modeled oneness and interdependence. Jesus shared that he was (and still is) one with the Father, and they work in community: "I and the Father are one" (John 10:30, 38; 14:10; 17:11, 22). Believers encounter God through God incarnate, God becoming flesh, Immanuel, Jesus Christ—God with us. Not only is Jesus one with the Father, but during His earthly ministry He also lived a life in community with the twelve.

Additionally, Jesus redefined family by making it clear that family was not identified by biological ties only. He challenged His followers to reconsider their loyalty to their families:

> Do not suppose that I have come to bring peace to the earth. I did not come to bring peace, but a sword. For I have come to turn a man against his father, a daughter against her mother, a daughter-in-law against her mother-in-law—a man's enemies will be the members of his own household. Anyone who loves his father or mother more than me is not worthy of me; anyone who loves his son or daughter more than me is not worthy of me; and anyone who does not take his cross and follow me is not worthy of me (Matt. 10:34-38).

Not only did Jesus redefine family relationships, but in the Gospels, He also modeled the preeminence of spiritual relationships. He asked, "Who are my mother and my brothers?" (Mark 3:33). He then looked at those who surrounded Him and said, "Here are my mother and my brothers! Whoever does God's will, is my brother and sister and mother" (Mark 3:34-35). In addition, Jesus referred to His followers as "brothers" (Matt. 23:8; 25:40; Luke 8:21; John 21:23; Rom. 8:29; Heb. 2:11, 17; Rev. 12:10; 19:10).

The early church was a spiritual community and family. It is said of the apostles of the early church that, "every day they continued to meet together in the temple courts. They broke bread in their homes and ate together with glad and sincere hearts" (Acts 2:46). In addition to worshipping together, the early church also fellowshipped together. They ministered to one another's needs: "All the believers were together and had everything in common. Selling their possessions and goods, they gave to anyone as he had need" (Acts 2:33-34). They viewed themselves as a whole rather than individuals; they were community.

Jesus laid down His majesty in order to serve humanity as He modeled community through service to others. He taught that those who aspired to become great would not exercise authority over others but would humble themselves and serve (Matt. 20:25-27). His earthly life was given to service (Matt. 20:28; Luke 22:27). As He was nearing the end of His earthly ministry, He humbly washed the disciples' feet (John 13:1-5), again demonstrating what true service to others looked like. Jesus gave everything for others, including His life. He said,

> Whoever wants to become great among you must be your servant, and whoever wants to be first must be slave of all. For even the Son of Man did not come to be served, but to serve, and to give his life as a ransom for many (Mark 10:43-45).

The apostle Paul exhorted the Philippians to follow Christ's example of humility and servanthood. He stated,

> Your attitude should be the same as that of Christ Jesus: Who, being in very nature God, did not consider equality with God something to be grasped, but made himself nothing, taking the very nature of a servant, being made in human likeness. And being found in appearance as a man, he humbled himself and became obedient to death –even death on a cross! (Phil. 2:5-8)

Additionally, when Jesus' earthly ministry was ending, He assured His followers that He would not leave them alone. He had been in community with them, and soon He would send another to dwell with them; the third person of the Trinity, the Holy Spirit, would be their comforter, helper, advocate, and so much more (John 14-16). Jesus, therefore, was a demonstration of life in community with others through relationships, humility, service, and presence.

Believers Need Community

Within the context of community individuals can become all that God intends for them to be. When we understand God's intentions for community, we begin to see the value of an intentional commitment to others for the purpose of spiritual formation. Bill Donahue and Russ Robinson explain that being created in the image of God meant more than men and women being created with a soul, but that "God chose to embed in us a distinct kind of relational DNA. God created us all with a 'community gene,' an inborn, intentional, inescapable part of what it means to be human."[67] A believer cannot experience optimal spiritual growth without community. Tony Evans writes,

> Why do fish travel in schools? Why do birds fly in formation? Why do cattle move in herds? Hyenas move in packs? Because

they understand that they cannot reach their maximum potential apart from the group. Lions prey on animals that stray from the group. Bears look for fish that are no longer moving with the school.... As is true for the animal kingdom, the mammal kingdom, it is true for the kingdom of God. Maximum growth cannot occur apart from the community.[68]

When we live independently of each other, we eliminate the very pathway God intended for our spiritual growth and development. The Christian experience is not to be lived out in isolation—it is to be nurtured in community.

Small Groups and a Sense of Community

In reference to small groups, Eddie Mosley, pastor of LifePoint Church in Smyrna, Tennessee, states,

In a small group, people study the Bible together and discuss the issues and challenges of life. They pray, care for one another, and are missed if they don't show up. Friendships form. Small groups transform a large church into a small, intimate congregation. Small groups are organic in nature. That means they operate more as a family, with issues, time constraints, and changes constantly occurring in the lives of their members.[69]

A great benefit of small group discipleship is that it builds community. Small groups can have a powerful impact on individual lives, families, and the faith community as a whole. No matter how large a local church may be, small groups enable the church to become a close-knit, intimate spiritual community. Small groups enable people to engage in life together and are a place where intimate relationships can be formed. They foster true community, and true community provides strength for life's storms, support for life's challenges, godly counsel for making important decisions, accountability, friendship, and acceptance. This is what true community is all about. It involves existing in relationship with others.

Summary

God has always existed in community. Jesus' earthly ministry provided an example of living within the context of community. We were created to be in community with God and with others. Small group discipleship fosters a sense of community that cannot be experienced within the context of the larger faith community. Small groups serve to unify a body of individuals. They provide a sense of connection that being a part of a larger congregation cannot provide. They connect people at the heart and enable accountability, belonging, and care. As a result, they link people together where relationships can be formed, and lives can be transformed.

QUESTIONS TO PONDER

1) As a member of your church, do you feel like a lone ranger, or do you feel a sense of community and belonging? What has attributed to your answer?

2) What steps will you take personally, as a church member, or as a church leader to create a sense of community in your life and in the lives of others?

[64]Paul Pavao, "The Council of Nicea: Part III," *Christian History for Everyman,* accessed October 16, 2014, http://www.christian-history.org/council-of-nicea-3.html.

[65]William G. Rusch, ed., *The Trinitarian Controversy: Sources of Early Christian Thought* (Philadelphia: Fortress Press, 1980), 2.

[66]M. Turner and G. McFarlane, "Trinity," *New Bible Dictionary,* 3rd ed., ed. by D. R. W. Wood et al. (Downers Grove, Ill.: InterVarsity Press, 1996), 1211.

[67]Bill Donahue and Russ Robinson, *Building a Church of Small Groups: A Place Where Nobody Stands Alone* (Grand Rapids: Zondervan, 2001), 24.

[68]Tony Evans, foreword to *A Practical Guide for Christian Discipleship and Mentoring* by Wanda Bolton-Davis (Cedar Hill, Tex.: Victorious Disciples Publishing, 2014), 11.

[69]Eddie Mosely, *Connecting in Communities: Understanding the Dynamics of Small Groups* (Colorado Springs: NavPress, 2011), 15.

CHAPTER SEVEN

It Is About the Kingdom:
Participating in the Mission of God

Defining the Mission of God

I DEFINE the mission of God as God's ultimate goal and plan of redemption for all creation, and the calling He has on every believer's life to co-labor with Him in accomplishing that goal—all for His glory. This involves utilizing the gifts, knowledge, talents, strengths, and resources that God has given to every believer, to represent and reflect the glory of God in their homes, communities, to the ends of the earth, and every place in between.

The Bible clearly reveals the passion of God for His own glory (Is. 48:9-11). In his book, *Mission of God,* Christopher Wright states,

> "There is one God at work in the universe and in human history, and that God has a goal, a purpose, a mission that will ultimately be accomplished by the power of God's Word and for the glory of God's name. This is the mission of the biblical God."[70]

Every disciple of Jesus Christ has a specific calling and an assigned responsibility in the *missio Dei* (mission of God). Disciples of Jesus

Christ are called to honor God by reclaiming everything for the glory of God. We are called to co-labor with God in his mission to take the whole Gospel to the whole world.

This task involves two components: first, it involves understanding the kingdom of God; and second, it involves being a witness.

Understanding the Kingdom of God

The kingdom of God is God's comprehensive rule and reign over all creation and in the hearts of believers. It is God's government, which involves His rulership and dominion over heaven and earth. The kingdom of God is past, present, and future and is experienced by all believers who allow God to rule and reign in their lives. Believers have dual citizenship. We live in this world, but we are governed by God's order. This dualism is seen in the synoptic Gospels. Jesus' teachings on the kingdom of God embodied a contrast between the present age and the age to come. The apostle Paul writes, "Do not conform any longer to the pattern of this world but be transformed by the renewing of your mind. Then you will be able to test and approve what God's will is—his good, pleasing and perfect will" (Rom. 12:2). We live on earth, but our citizenship is in the kingdom of heaven.

Jesus makes it clear that those who belong to Him are in this world but are not of this world (John 15:19; 17:6, 9, 11, 14-18). God desires to manifest His glorious character, wisdom, righteous judgments, and purposes in the earthly realm. God has chosen to accomplish this through His people. Just as Jesus' earthly ministry was committed to the will of the Father (John 5:19; 8:28), so must every Christian be faithful to the mandate of establishing God's will on earth as it is in heaven (Matt. 6:10; 18:18-20). Myles Munroe states,

> Kingdom citizenship is about recognizing our place and rights through Christ as citizens of God's Kingdom, and claiming

those rights so that we can fulfill God's Kingdom purpose in our world. It is about taking over again that which once was lost because of our sin and disobedience. Our Kingdom faith is about claiming and living out our dominion mandate.[71]

In order to participate in the mission of God, believers must understand that they are not only Christians and disciples of Jesus Christ, but they are also citizens of the kingdom of God and thus, there is a kingdom mandate on their lives. The kingdom of God is the primary theme of the New Testament (Luke 16:16). John the Baptist prepared the way of the Lord with the message, "Repent, for the kingdom of heaven is near" (Matt. 3:2). Later, Jesus Christ the Messiah came on the scene, and during His public ministry He preached one message: the kingdom. He said, "Repent, for the kingdom of heaven is near" (Matt. 4:17; Mark 1:15). He often taught on the subject of what "the Kingdom of Heaven is like" (Matt. 13:24, 31, 44, 47). No doubt, the kingdom of God was Jesus' priority, and it should be ours as well. Jesus preached and taught the kingdom. It was the foundation for everything He did. Matthew records Jesus as saying, "But seek first his kingdom and his righteousness, and all these things will be given to you as well" (Matt. 6:33). The kingdom of God was Jesus' life focus and message.

Jesus commissioned His followers to take the gospel of the kingdom to the ends of the earth, saying, "And this gospel of the kingdom will be preached in the whole world as a testimony to all nations, and then the end will come" (Matt. 24:14). The book of Acts records how Jesus' followers continued with the message of the kingdom. Empowered by the Holy Spirit, many who heard their message were baptized. Luke, the beloved physician, writes, "But when they believed Philip as he preached the good news of the kingdom of God and the name of Jesus Christ, they were baptized, both men and women" (Acts 8:12).

Later, the apostle Paul taught the early church about the kingdom (Acts 28:23).

John the Baptist, Jesus, Peter, Paul, and the other apostles not only preached about the kingdom, but they died for the kingdom. After the apostles were martyred, the torch of the Great Commission (Matt. 28:19) was passed on to the next generation of Jesus' disciples and continues to be passed on to every believer today. It is the gospel message of the kingdom of heaven that still compels men, women, boys, and girls to repent, be baptized, and preach Jesus the Christ, preparing the way for the Lord's second coming.

Being a Witness

Those whom God employs, He qualifies and empowers for service. As Jesus was nearing the end of His earthly ministry, He ensured the disciples, now called apostles (Acts 1:2), that they would be spiritually equipped for the task ahead of them. He said, "You will receive power when the Holy Spirit comes on you; and you will be my witnesses in Jerusalem, and in all Judea and Samaria, and to the ends of the earth" (Acts 1:8). This power was the soon-to-come Holy Spirit whom they would experience on the day of Pentecost (Acts 2:1-4). They would not be able to accomplish the mission that was before them in their own strength. They would be filled with the Holy Spirit who would empower them for a worldwide campaign.

Jesus' words, "be my witnesses," also involved proclamation of the good news (1 Cor. 15:1-4). The good news was the gospel, "the power of God for the salvation to everyone who believes: first for the Jew, then for the Gentile" (Rom. 1:16). The good news of the gospel was to be proclaimed throughout the world (Matt. 24:14; Mark 13:10; Luke 24:47). The gospel message was the story of Jesus and was to be understood in light of the Old Testament. The gospel message of justification

(Rom. 4:25; 5:1, 9; Gal. 3:8), salvation (John 1:12; 3:16; Rom. 6:23, Eph. 2:8), reconciliation (Rom. 5:10: 2 Cor. 5:18-21; Col. 1:20), forgiveness (Is. 1:18: Eph. 1:7; 1 John 1:9), redemption (Ps. 111:9; 1 Cor. 1:30; Eph. 1:7), and new life in the Spirit (Rom. 8:11; 2 Cor. 5:17; Eph. 2:6) was to be proclaimed, heard, believed, and received as truth (Rom. 10:17).

The apostles had been taught by Jesus, had witnessed His earthly ministry, and had observed His suffering, death, and resurrection. This qualified them to be His witnesses (Luke 24:45-48; Acts 1:21-22). As Jesus' earthly ministry came to an end, their task was to make the gospel known through word and deed. They would advance the kingdom by proclaiming Jesus as King, by preaching and publishing the truth of the gospel to the world. Their light would shine from Judea to Samaria and to the ends of the earth. They would confirm their testimony with divine miracles and supernatural gifts. They would become martyrs, bearing witness to the truth with their sufferings and even their lives.

The mandate to bear witness was not only directed to the New Testament apostles, but the charge is also extended to every believer today. Jesus' vision was that the witnessing work of His ministry and community would continue beyond the first generation of eyewitnesses to the ongoing testimony of those who would later come to faith in Him. Therefore, every disciple of Jesus Christ today has the same mission and mandate as the apostles—to make the gospel known in all the earth.

Kingdom Living

Kingdom citizenship entails living with a kingdom worldview and engaging the world from a kingdom perspective. God's ways and principles will not only confront the ways of the world, but they will directly contradict them. Jesus' teaching challenged the world system on many levels (Matt. 10:34-42; Mark 7:6-23). Jesus' philosophy was countercultural and directly conflicted with the laws and principles of that day (Matt. 5-7; Luke 6:20-49). Because God and His Word are unchanging, this truth remains today. The Bible will forever confront and conflict with the world system. When Christians make the commitment to live and address world issues according to biblical principles, they will encounter opposition from the world system. This explains why all disciples of Jesus Christ, both historically and at present, experience opposition, suffering, and even persecution (Luke 6:22; 2 Cor. 4:8-12).

If the prophets, the disciples, and Jesus were persecuted, then persecution is inevitable for every believer who follows Jesus' teachings. Paul tells Timothy, "Everyone who wants to live a godly life in Christ Jesus will be persecuted" (2 Tim. 3:12b). Jesus said,

> If the world hates you, keep in mind that it hated me first. If you belonged to the world, it would love you as its own. As it is, you do not belong to the world, but I have chosen you out of the world. That is why the world hates you. Remember the words I spoke to you: "No servant is greater than his master." If they persecuted me, they will persecute you also (John 15:18-20).

Jesus warned that the world hated Him first and would also hate His followers. This would only be an indication that they did not belong to the world. Jesus later said, "I have told you these things, so that in me you may have peace. In this world you will have trouble, but take heart! I have overcome the world" (John 16:33). Matthew Henry writes, "He [Jesus] comforts them with a promise of peace in him, by virtue of his victory over the world, whatever troubles they might meet within it."[72] Every believer can find hope in knowing that although suffering and persecution are inevitable, victory is promised (Rom. 8:17; 36; 2 Cor. 1:7, 11:23; Phil. 3:10). Paul assures Timothy, "If we died with him, we will also live with him; if we endure, we will also reign with him" (2 Tim. 2:11-12).

This commitment to live in the world in accordance to God's kingdom principles can be reflected to an unsaved world and make an impact in the world for the glory of God. Petersen writes,

> Whatever we may be doing—caring for our homes, discipling our children, meeting a deadline for our boss, or taking a vacation—we need to remember that we are at the same time making a statement about what it means to belong to God.[73]

Our daily actions and interactions in the world make a pronounced statement about what it means to live in relationship with Jesus as a kingdom citizen. This is what it means to be light and salt of the earth (Matt. 5:13-16).

Small Groups and Participation in the Mission of God

Small group discipleship can be a means of helping people learn to integrate sharing their faith into the normal ongoing flow of the relationships they already have at home, in the community, in the business world, locally, globally, and wherever they may be. This can foster an environment that opens the door for individuals to join God in His work of making Himself known to a dying world.

Small groups help people confront challenges, and they teach an alternative way of engaging the world. As a result, a culture is created where discipleship forms kingdom-minded people who engage the world from a biblical worldview, and who impact the world around them as they join God in his redemptive mission. Discipleship helps individuals learn that they are fulfilling a greater purpose—the expansion of Christ's kingdom. It helps them understand they are not simply members of a local church, but they belong to a greater church, whose purpose is to establish the kingdom of God. As a result, whatever we do, we are aiming to live fully in the kingdom of God, now, here, and hereafter.

Small group discipleship is not a new phenomenon. Somehow with time, this effective method of making disciples of Jesus Christ has almost been lost. The church does not need to search for new ideas for maturing believers in the faith. We need only look at the foundation that has already been laid. Today's church leaders often seek to implement new programs and events to invite people into a relationship with Jesus and form them into disciples. However, we may need only to look to our spiritual ancestors and church leaders for a biblical model to make small group discipleship an effective place for faith formation, learning, and transformation.

Summary

Discipleship helps people locate themselves in God's story so they may co-labor with Him to achieve His purposes for His glory. In *Experiencing God*, Henry Blackaby, Richard Blackaby, and Claude King assert that once a believer has an intimate relationship with God, his or her job is to "watch to see where God is at work and join him."[74] Being strategic and intentional through small group discipleship fosters an environment where individuals do not only grow in their knowledge of God's Word and develop lives of obedience, but they also come to understand where and how they fit into God's big picture of fulfilling His mission. When we as believers come to understand the kingdom of God and what it means to be a witness, we join God is His work as an active participant in fulfilling His mission.

QUESTIONS TO PONDER

1) What is your understanding of the Kingdom of God? How do you see yourself being involved in God's redemptive mission? What part has God assigned to you?

2) How will you help others discover their part in God's redemptive mission?

---

[70]Christopher Wright, *Mission of God: Unlocking the Bible's Grand Narrative* (Downers Grove, Ill.: InterVarsity, 2006), 64.

[71]Myles Munroe, *Applying the Kingdom: Rediscovering the Priority of God for Mankind* (Shippensburg, Penna.: Destiny Image, 2007), 60.

[72]Matthew Henry, *Matthew Henry's Commentary on the Whole Bible: Complete and Unabridged in One Volume* (Peabody, Mass.: Hendrickson, 1994), 2027.

[73]Jim Petersen, *Lifestyle Discipleship: The Challenge of Following Jesus in Today's World* (Colorado Springs: NavPress, 1993), 175.

[74]Blackaby, Blackaby, and King, *Experiencing God*, 44.

Laying a Solid Foundation:
Spiritual Growth Path

Spiritual Growth Path

BEGINNING WITH a Spiritual Growth Path (SGP) will help lay a solid foundation for implementing small groups. A SGP is a strategic blueprint designed to guide believers in their spiritual growth and development. A SGP accomplishes two goals. First, it provides Christians with a road map for spiritual growth. Second, the SGP provides churches with a consistent leadership pipeline. Without a consistent method of developing spiritually mature leaders, a church will die. It is no different than with any other organism—when it ceases to produce, it becomes extinct. When new leaders are not consistently growing and being produced within the church, the current leaders eventually burn out, become dull, irrelevant, or ineffective. Additionally, a major advantage of an SGP is that it enables churches to produce leaders from within who understand the church's vision, mission, and processes.

The SGP should be clearly communicated and made available to every church member. It should be deeply embedded within the church's culture. It is to be communicated from the time a person becomes a new member and continues to be communicated throughout the church on an ongoing basis. Everyone should know what the SGP is. It should be emphasized from the senior leadership, church staff, ministry leaders, and volunteers. This can be reinforced verbally on the church's website, through graphics posted throughout the church, through emails, and any other communication vehicles. The SGP sends the message that not only is spiritual growth an expectation, but it is also a priority.

I propose that the SGP include four vital phases. These include:

Phase 1: Making Disciples

Phase 2: Maturing Disciples

Phase 3: Multiplying Disciples

Phase 4: Mobilizing Disciples.

These four phases lay a foundation for a solid assimilation process, and clearly outline how members can immediately get connected and involved in the discipling process from the time they become members of the church.

Phase 1: Making Disciples

Phase 1 is about making disciples and focuses on getting people connected. Many church leaders refer to this initial step in the assimilation process as the new member orientation phase. As new converts and new members come to your church, you will want to get them *connected* as soon as possible.

Notice I did not say, you will want to get them *involved*. There is a distinction, and too often church leaders seek to get people involved immediately, only to learn later that their involvement was premature. However, getting new people connected as quickly as possible is vitally important. The retention of new members is highly associated with making them feel a sense of connection to the ministry, and not so much as overwhelming them with various tasks. Engaging them in orientation, teaching and training before they get deeply involved will be well worth the time and investment. Some suggested topics you may want to include in your new member orientation curriculum include the following:

- Baptism, Assurance of Salvation and Identity in Christ
- Evangelism: Sharing Your Salvation Story
- The Priesthood of all Believers
- How to Study the Bible
- Worship
- The Holy Spirit
- Gifts of the Spirit and Spiritual Gift Inventory
- Discipleship
- Spiritual Disciplines
- Stewardship
- Your Church's Vision, Mission and Core Values
- Doctrinal Beliefs
- Church Ordinances

You may want to cover this information and other topics of your choice within several sessions, over a period of days or weeks.

Phase 2: Maturing Disciples

Phase 2 involves helping an individual begin the journey of being

a lifelong disciple of Jesus Christ. This phase entails developing disciples for ministry and maturity through intentional discipleship. This phase offers two primary opportunities. The first opportunity is for spiritual growth through participation in a discipleship small group. Spiritually mature and trained small group facilitators should always be readily available to welcome new members into a small group. Not only is getting people connected vitally important but keeping them connected is equally as important. As discussed in chapter 6, small group discipleship provides a sense of community and belonging which fosters an environment for meaningful relationships that can aid in spiritual growth. You cannot always depend upon individuals to take the initiative to enroll in a small group. Therefore, it is suggested that you include at the end of Phase 1 an easy way for people to onboard Phase 2. An effortless registration process, email reminders and even the personal touch of a phone call from a staff person, volunteer, or small group facilitator will go a long way in keeping people on track.

Secondly, in addition to getting connected in a small group, phase 2 provides an opportunity for members to get involved by volunteering in various areas of the church such as hospitality, outreach, community events, ministry events, etc. These non-leadership positions not only provide an opportunity for individuals to serve, but they also provide the opportunity for them to discover their spiritual gifts and serve in that capacity.

Additionally, you may want to consider training your volunteers. Volunteer training is extremely important in creating the culture that reflects the vision and mission of the church. Volunteer training increases consistency in service, increases the confidence of your volunteers, helps volunteers feel valued, and provide you an opportunity to observe integrity, character, and identify potential leaders. This is also a good time in the SGP process to utilize my discipleship workbook entitled, *Victorious Disciples: A Practical Guide to Christian Discipleship and Mentoring*.[75] Additional training topics you might incorporate in this phase include giving, stewardship, spiritual gifts, spiritual disciplines and serving.

Phase 3: Multiplying Disciples

Phase 3 is a continuation of Phase 2 and involves equipping disciples on a deeper level. Not only are you equipping disciples, but you are developing leaders. In this phase you are equipping disciples to make disciples. This phase is absolutely important, and as with all the other phases, it is crucial for the vitality of your church. When you find a church that is stagnant, apathetic, or declining, it bears the necessity to assess their leadership development process. To disciple is to multiply, and to multiply is to develop leaders.

Phase 3 entails the continuation of spiritual growth. As people continue on the journey of discipleship, transformation and growth is inevitable. As discussed in Chapter 5, you will want to make spiritual growth outcomes available so that members may assess their own growth and development. They may evaluate themselves in the following areas:

- Am I displaying a lifestyle as a disciple?
- Am I sharing the gospel on a consistent basis?
- Am I displaying spiritual maturity through faith, prayer, and the fruit of the Spirit as described in Galatians 5:20-22?
- Am I discipling others?
- Am I demonstrating effective leadership abilities?
- Do I minister to others?
- Do I fellowship with other believers?
- Do I abide in the Word?

These and other questions can serve as a means of personal evaluation for your members as you equip them on their spiritual journey.

Phase 3 also focuses on developing and equipping leaders for service.

Being ineffective in this phase can cause a shortage of capable leaders within the church. This can happen when new leaders are not being developed and also when there is no leadership rotation in place for long-term leaders. Phase 3 ensures the consistent training of new leaders to replace current leaders.

I have witnessed leaders serving in the same capacity for thirty and forty years, and sometimes they even die in the position. While their commitment is to be commended, even in the secular world, a time comes when retirement is recommended. When a leader is declining and continues to serve "until death do us part," it can cause the ministry to die long before, or along with, the lifelong leader. As a result, the leader's demise can leave behind a ministry, along with people, who have lost momentum and become stagnant and dormant. Every leader should have a succession plan and a prospective successor; this includes the lead pastor. This is the biblical model as seen with Moses and Joshua, Elijah and Elisha, and even Jesus and the Holy Spirit.

When functioning properly, this phase should produce strong, impactful, spiritually mature leaders. It should provide a leadership pipeline for the church, the local community, and beyond. This phase serves to equip leaders for service both within the local church, as well as outside of the church. Specific classes can be offered to train and prepare individuals for leadership in specialized areas. Training topics might include evangelism, discipleship, Bible courses, leadership, and Christian living. The goal in this phase is to raise up faithful disciple-making disciples and impactful leaders for the kingdom.

Phase 4: Mobilizing Disciples

Phase 4, Mobilizing Disciples, involves deploying individuals. This phase produces kingdom ambassadors who are equipped to minister to others and witness to the world. They are life-changing catalysts and make an impact in their sphere of influence. They engage in purposeful leadership and understand that ministry is not limited within the church and is not divided into spiritual and secular, but everything is ministry. By now they have learned that they are called to participate in the mission of God within every sphere of influence, to include family, religion, government, education, social media, arts and entertainment, and entrepreneurship.

Ongoing training is offered at a more specialized and intense level. Training areas might include discipleship and evangelism with a focus on missions, Bible and Theology, Christian Living, and Leadership, which includes the choice of two components: First, church ministry, for those who are called to ministry within the church (i.e., children's ministry, youth ministry, pastoring, church planting, worship ministry, church administration, teaching, preaching, etc.), and second, marketplace ministry, for those who are called to business and entrepreneurship. Keep in mind that these are only suggested areas of training. You can devise your own according to your needs.

The goal in Phase 4 is to equip individuals for the work of ministry and then mobilize and deploy them to do it. However, I must note that many times churches do well at equipping individuals but fail to deploy them. Not only do they fail to deploy their people, but it is not uncommon for church leaders to become upset after they have trained leaders and then those leaders feel led to leave and go someplace else to serve. However, deploying leaders is just as much a part of the discipleship process as discipling them. Jesus discipled the 12 in the Gospels, but in the book of Acts, they are no longer called disciples, but apostles. They were now being deployed and assigned the task of advancing the kingdom.

Mobilizing and deploying disciples is extremely important to strengthening the local church, multiplying disciples, building the body of Christ, and advancing the kingdom of God.

Summary

It is extremely important that Christians are not only being equipped, but that they are also being mobilized to serve. Having a well-developed Spiritual Growth Path will provide your church with a road map to help strategically disciple your people. A SGP helps give clear guidance for individuals on their spiritual journey. It provides the church with a means of equipping strong leaders on a continuous basis, thus providing a leadership pipeline for the church. Additionally, in order to be fully effective, the SGP must include a component that deploys Christians for service both inside and outside of the local church.

The four phases of the SGP we discussed in this chapter have been captured on the following diagrams. Diagrams 1 and 2 are examples of two ways to display the same Spiritual Growth Path. Diagram 2 utilizes graphics to demonstrate the phases. Using symbols to display your SGP can be effective and creative, as people learn to associate each phase with a picture. Both diagrams provide a clear, concise, easy to follow SGP, that can be displayed or given to members to provide them with a handy visual of the steps they will take toward spiritual growth.

These SGP diagrams are to serve as a guide for you to devise your own. The SGP should be tailored to fit your church's vision, mission, goals, training materials and capabilities. It should work and flow well for the culture of your church. Once the plan is created, it should be communicated on a continuous basis throughout the church, and shared with every new member as they become a part of your congregation.

Spiritual Growth Path (SGP)
(Diagram 1)

PHASE 1	PHASE 2
Making Disciples	*Maturing Disciples*

CONNECTING

- Baptism
- Workshop
- New member class
- Basics of Christianity
- Doctrinal beliefs
- Introduction to the church and church leaders

DISCIPLING

- Discipleship classes
- Small groups
- Volunteer training
- Serving
- Giving
- Stewardship
- Spiritual gifts
- Spiritual disciplines

PHASE 4	PHASE 3
Mobilizing Disciples	*Multiplying Disciples*

DEPLOYING

- Kingdom ambassador
- Ministering to others
- Witness to the world
- Specialized training
- Life-change catalyst
- Making an impact
- Purposeful leadership
- Participating in the mission of God

EQUIPPING

- Transformation and growth
- Displaying a lifestyle as a disciple
- Sharing the gospel
- Displaying spiritual maturity
- Making disciples
- Demonstrating leadership

Phase 1:
Making Disciples
CONNECTION

Phase 2:
Maturing Disciples
DISCIPLING

SPIRITUAL
GROWTH
PATH

Phase 4:
Mobilizing Disciples
DEPLOYING

Phase 3:
Multiplying Disciples
EQUIPPING

QUESTIONS TO PONDER

1) Does your church have a SGP? Is it being clearly communicated? Can you describe it? Is it effective? What would make it better?

---

[75]Wanda Bolton-Davis, *Victorious Disciples: A Practical Guide to Christian Discipleship and Mentoring* (Cedar Hill, Tex.: Victorious Disciples Publishing, 2004, 2014).

CHAPTER NINE

Let's Do It:
Implementing Small Groups in Your Church

Implementing or Enhancing Small Groups

THERE ARE six basic steps to implementing or enhancing small groups in your church, which include preparing, training, promoting, delegating, celebrating and evaluating.

Step One: Preparing

The first step in preparing to implement a small group discipleship ministry is prayer. Solely by God's grace will this ministry be implemented successfully. The leaders of this ministry are not merely being asked to volunteer their time, but they are being called to the ministry of disciple-making. Inviting the Holy Spirit to do a transforming work in all the hearts of those involved in launching this ministry is vitally important. Your prayers should encompass three primary areas: first, that God will send leaders who have a passion to disciple others; second, that God will send those who have a desire to be discipled; and third, that the Holy Spirit will work through all who are involved.

I cannot express the importance of prayer. If Jesus prayed before He chose the twelve (Luke 6:12-13), how much more is prayer necessary as you began this endeavor of small group discipleship.

After prayerful consideration, the next step is to identify and contact prospective discipleship small group facilitators. Inform them of the plan to begin small groups and ask them to pray about potentially being a small group facilitator. Schedule an introductory meeting where more information will be provided to see who a good fit for this ministry might be.

The third step is to initiate the administrative preparation necessary for assisting the progress of this ministry. These responsibilities would include preparing training materials for the facilitators, ordering the discipleship resources you have chosen to use, preparing any training handouts and PowerPoint slides, deciding upon meeting space, and reserving it if necessary.

Step Two: Training

Of the two steps within the training phase, the first is education, which involves a teaching session or sessions on the basics of discipleship. This might include defining specific terms related to discipleship, explaining the theological foundation for discipleship, casting the vision for the ministry, discussing the purpose of small groups, identifying biblical examples of discipleship, addressing the church's goal and mission, discussing the practical aspects of implementing small groups within the church, and addressing what it means to become effective disciple-makers and a small group facilitator. The *Victorious Disciples: A Practical Guide for Christian Discipleship and Mentoring Facilitator's Manual*[76] provides help to prepare and equip leaders for becoming disciple makers and facilitating small groups. This leadership guide includes lesson plans with goals and objectives for each lesson, administrative information, forms, and other details to aid them in being effective small group facilitators.

The second step within the training phase is demonstration. Ideally, the leaders who consent and commit to becoming a small group facilitator will agree to participate in a small group prior to leading one. Going through a small group before leading one has great benefits, particularly if these leaders have never been a part of a discipleship small group. The purpose of this part of the training is to engage the facilitators on a journey of personal spiritual formation and to model for them how to facilitate a small group. The study guide, *Victorious Disciples: A Practical Guide for Christian Discipleship and Mentoring*, can be utilized for the small group study.[77] The lessons include:

- ▶ "Knowing Who You Are in Christ"
- ▶ "How to Study the Bible"
- ▶ "The Journey of Faith"
- ▶ "Becoming a Prayer Warrior"
- ▶ "How to Fight the Battle and Win"
- ▶ "Love That Forgives"
- ▶ "Fasting for a Breakthrough"
- ▶ "Created for Worship"
- ▶ "Empowered by the Holy Spirit"
- ▶ "Becoming a Disciple Maker"

At the completion of their training, they are well on their way to implementing a small group discipleship ministry.

The following are a few of the facilitator criteria and expectations that should be considered when selecting the small group facilitators. These should be discussed during the initial training:

- A consistent prayer life
- A good steward of God's resources (time, talent and treasure)
- Biblical knowledge and a consistent study of the Word
- A godly lifestyle demonstrated by Christian character; being a person who operates with integrity, both privately and publicly
- Available to minister to participants as needed (listen, prayer, encourage, etc.)
- A willingness to be involved in a discipleship group as a participant
- A willingness to be transparent, sharing life experiences as appropriate

In addition to the previous list, a list of expectations for facilitators should also be communicated. Small group facilitators should:

- Have consistent attendance.
- Arrive early for group meetings to ensure the room is set up in a circle formation. (Being seated in a circle provides an atmosphere for intimacy and sharing.)
- Arrive to each group meeting prepared to lead the discussion of the lesson.
- Facilitate the group through dialogue versus teaching the lesson.
- Be cognizant of quiet individuals in the group and invite them into the discussion, while gently redirecting overly talkative individuals.
- Begin and end each session in a timely manner.
- Follow up with group members regularly (weekly/biweekly), especially those who express prayer needs.

The small group training not only prepares leaders to facilitate small groups, but it also serves to deepen their personal discipleship with Jesus. It is important that their personal discipleship with Jesus is strengthened before they begin to lead others. Even if small group facilitator training is for only eight to ten weeks, involving your new facilitators in a small group prior to releasing them to lead one will have tremendous value.

Step Three: Promoting

After the leaders engage in preparation through prayer and training, if you have not already begun to do so, it is time to begin to inform the membership (church-wide) of the new small group ministry. The pastor might begin to preach and teach on discipleship. This is a great time to preach a series on discipleship. A sermon series with an impactful title (i.e., "Next Level Discipleship") will serve to educate the church membership about discipleship, help cast the vision, and unify the church in implementing this new ministry. This time can be very exciting for the church as you prepare to introduce a ministry that will literally impact the trajectory of the lives of the people in your church.

The trained leaders will also serve as catalyst to inform and inspire others. You might enlist their help to pass out flyers, assist with registration, etc. Feel free to check out our discipleship accessories, such as t-shirts, buttons, etc. on our website, that help to increase interest, curiosity, and momentum for the small groups. Additionally, registration can be made available after your worship service on Sunday and throughout the week. Registration can also be offered online if you have digital capability.

Step Four: Delegating

This phase involves delegating the responsibility of facilitating the small groups to the leadership team who have now completed training. Following the registration period, you may want to host a gathering such as a breakfast or luncheon for those who registered. This gathering will serve to prepare everyone for the launching of the groups. At this event, you will want to inform, instruct, introduce, and ignite.

- **Inform.** Provide an abbreviated presentation of the vision for disciple making. This should not be new information but should reinforce what the pastor has been teaching and preaching.

- **Instruct.** Provide pertinent information about the specifics of the ministry, i.e., the structure, time, and place where the small group sessions will be held.

- **Introduce.** Provide an opportunity for the participants to meet their small group facilitators.

- **Ignite.** Make the gathering a fun-filled time. Let it inspire the participants to look forward to beginning a journey of spiritual development with each other.

Step Five: Celebrating

At the completion of specific milestones of the SGP, there should be a celebration. This celebration can be tailored to fit your congregation. It can be as formal as a graduation ceremony or as informal as a picnic. It can be during morning worship service or a separate event. The important thing is that you celebrate the spiritual successes in the lives of those who participated. A certificate or some sort of memorabilia will have lasting meaning. The purpose of this ceremony is not to acknowledge the end or the completion of their commitment, but rather to celebrate the beginning of a lifetime commitment to discipleship.

You might include testimonials of the life-transforming work that occurred in individuals' lives as a result of following Jesus. There will be many stories of how God changed lives through the study of the Word and through newfound relationships. This celebration will serve to encourage the participants and others to persevere in their relationship with Jesus. Additionally, this celebration allows the church members to share in the celebration, to hear the testimonies and also be inspired to get involved in a small group.

Step Six: Evaluating

After you have gone through the previous 5 steps of implementing or enhancing small groups in your church, it is important to evaluate the ministry on an on-going basis. You will want to assess each step in the implementation process to ensure each phase was executed in the most efficient manner. Additionally, you will want to evaluate three primary areas. These areas include the following:

I. The processes and infrastructure of the ministry

    A. Is the structure and overall framework of the ministry well organized? Are there any loopholes? Do you have the right people in the right place?

    B. Did the registration process flow well? Is it easy for people to get connected in a group? Are there any obstacles?

    C. Did the training process go well? How can it be improved? Were the facilitators well prepared? What additional information might you consider including in the next training session?

    D. Is the ministry growing? (Discipleship involves multiplication.)

II. The ministry leaders / group facilitators

    A. What are the strengths of the ministry leaders/facilitators? What are their weaknesses?

    B. Are the leaders/facilitators fulfilling their duties as assigned?

    C. Do they feel adequately prepared to facilitate a group?

    D. What additional support might you provide for the ministry leaders/facilitators to assist with their spiritual growth?

III. The small group participants

    A. Is the small group experience meeting their expectations? What would make it better?

    B. Are the participants attending regularly and are they engaged in the group?

    C. Are their lives being impacted and transformed?

    D. Are personal testimonies of lifestyle changes being shared?

    E. Are the participants becoming disciple makers?

    F. Are they serving and utilizing their spiritual gifts? Are you providing opportunities for them serve?

    G. Are they being developed into leaders?

Of course, this list of questions is not exhaustive and can be expanded. These questions are to get you started. Remember, evaluating your discipleship ministry should be done on an ongoing basis, so prepare to be flexible and open to change.

Summary

Discipleship is not magical, nor is the specific method of small group discipleship magical. However, Jesus taught discipleship, modeled small group discipleship, and commissioned believers to make disciples. We are being commissioned to the work of making disciples as Jesus did. Neither discipleship nor the discipling method of small groups ensures the transformation of the heart. However, both serve as a method that can guide people toward opening their hearts to the transforming power of the Holy Spirit. This is why everyone involved (the pastor, church leaders, staff, small group leaders, and small group participants) must commit to prayer and yield to the power of the Holy Spirit; only then will lives be changed. The apostle John writes, "The Spirit gives life; the flesh counts for nothing" (John 6:63a).

QUESTIONS TO PONDER

1) Does your church currently offer discipleship small groups? What is your role (i.e. participant, facilitator, ministry leader, church staff, pastor)? Are your small groups effective? What would make them better?

2) Does your church provide regular training and support for your small group facilitators?

[76]Wanda Bolton-Davis, *Victorious Disciples: A Practical Guide for Christian Discipleship and Mentoring Facilitator's Manual*, a manual prepared for discipleship training given by Victorious Disciples Ministries, Inc., 2009.

[77]Wanda Bolton-Davis, *Victorious Disciples: A Practical Guide for Christian Discipleship and Mentoring* (Enumclaw, Wa: Pleasant Word, 2004).

CHAPTER TEN

The Charge:
Returning to the Great Commission

WE HAVE discussed the spiritual problem of non-discipleship and how it has impeded the spiritual growth of Christians. As a result, the local church and the body of Christ is experiencing a disciple deficit. The shortage of authentic disciples being produced has vast consequences and implications within the church and within the world. Christianity appears to be losing ground in the midst of a prevailing immoral world. As a result, we examined the need for churches to implement a discipleship strategy whereby church members are intentionally and effectively discipled.

The biblical mission of the church is to make disciples. While most Christians are familiar with the mandate of discipleship found in the New Testament through the Great Commission (Matt. 28:19-20), there is also the concept of discipleship found in the Old Testament. This informs us that discipleship is deeply rooted in God's plan, as well as His method for maturing and growing believers for His glory.

As a result, discipleship should be the foundation and fulcrum of the church. From the assimilation of new members and throughout every ministry of the church, discipleship is the filter through which everything should operate. Discipling relationships are fundamental and can lead people to Christ, help believers grow in Christ and help mature believers develop into great leaders.

Pastors, church staff, church leaders, seminary professors, students, lay leaders, and every believer hold the responsibility to address the problem of non-discipleship. This book proposes that an effective way to contend with the disciple deficit is through small group discipleship. Among the many benefits of small group discipleship, my research demonstrates that individuals who participate in a discipleship small group will experience a measurable increase in spiritual growth, a sense of community, and participation in the mission of God. Spiritual growth is optimized when a spiritual growth path is in place and when spiritual growth outcomes are clearly communicated. A sense of community is created among individuals when they come together in a small group that includes trust, grace, humility, affirmation, and accountability, while committed to forming authentic relationships. Small groups enable the local church to become a close-knit, intimate spiritual community. Small groups foster participation in the mission of God as individuals learn what it means to co-labor with God and join God in His work to advance the kingdom of God for His glory.

I encourage pastors, church staff, church leaders, and seminary professors to assess their method of making disciples by asking the following questions:

1) Is making disciples the priority for our ministry?

2) Are we being intentional in making disciples?

3) What strategy do we have in place for making disciples?

4) Do we have a Spiritual Growth Path available to our church members?

5) Can our church members articulate our strategy for making disciples?

6) Do we provide spiritual growth outcomes that allow our members to assess their personal spiritual growth and development?

7) How do we measure whether we are being successful in making disciples?

8) Do we have a leadership pipeline whereby we are effectively and continuously developing strong, spiritually mature leaders?

9) Are we mobilizing and deploying leaders?

Additionally, the following questions may be asked of seminary professors:

10) Are we adequately preparing seminary students to be committed followers of Jesus Christ?

11) Have we equipped our seminary students with the tools they need to implement an effect discipleship process within the context of their ministry?

The theological foundation for discipleship has been laid before us, the clarion call to make disciples has been extended to us, and the need to raise up mature disciples is all around us. As church leaders and believers, we are being summoned and charged to return to the Great Commission. What is your response?

QUESTIONS TO PONDER

1) How will you use what you have learned to strengthen your personal discipleship to Jesus? How will you use the information gained from this book to strengthen discipleship in your church and in the world?

2) What are your next steps to return to the Great Commission? How will you put what you have learned into action?

3) How can Victorious Disciples Ministries help take your personal discipleship and the discipleship ministry in your church to the next level?

Other Books by Dr. Wanda Bolton-Davis

Available on Amazon

Victorious Disciples:
A Practical Guide to Christian Discipleship and Mentoring

Victorious Disciples:
A Practical Guide to Christian Discipleship and Mentoring
Facilitator's Manual

The Victorious Life 30-Day Devotional

Contact Information

Address:
P.O. Box 1803 • Cedar Hill, TX 75106

Website: www.wandaboltondavis.com
Email: drwanda@wandaboltondavis.com

Recommended Resources

Carbonell, Mel and Stanley R. Ponz. *Uniquely You Membership & Ministry Profile.* Blue Ridge, Ga.: Uniquely You Resources, 2006.

Foster, Richard J. *Celebration of Discipline: The Path to Spiritual Growth.* New York: HarperCollins, 1978, 1988, 1998.

Bibliography

Barna, George. *Growing True Disciples: New Strategies for Producing Genuine Followers of Christ.* Colorado Springs: Waterbrook Press, 2001.

Barron, Candace. "Small Group Theology: Part One," October 31, 2013. The Network for Discipleship and Mission, United Methodists of Arkansas. Accessed October 9, 2014. http://network.arumc.org/spiritual-formation/small-group-theology-part-1, 3.

Blackaby, Henry, Richard Blackaby, and Claude V. King. *Experiencing God: How to Live the Full Adventure of Knowing and Doing the Will of God.* Nashville: Broadman and Holman, 1994.

Bolton-Davis, Wanda. "Evaluating the Effectiveness of Small Group Discipleship." DMin dissertation. Biola University Talbot School of Theology, 2015.

_____. *Victorious Disciples: A Practical Guide for Discipleship and Mentoring.* Enumclaw, WA: Pleasant Word, 2004, 2014.

_____. *Victorious Disciples: A Practical Guide for Christian Discipleship and Mentoring Facilitator's Guide.* Manual prepared for discipleship training by Victorious Disciples Ministries, 2009.

Boren, M. Scott. *Missiorelate: Becoming a Church of Missional Small Groups*. Houston: Touch Publications, 2011.

Bruce, Alexander Balmain. *Training the Twelve*. Memphis: General Books, 2009.

Carbonell, Mel and Stanley R. Ponz. *Uniquely You Membership & Ministry Profile*. Blue Ridge, Ga.: Uniquely You Resources, 2006.

Donahue, Bill and Russ Robinson. *Building a Church of Small Groups: A Place Where Nobody Stands Alone*. Grand Rapids: Zondervan, 2001.

Evans, Tony, foreword to *A Practical Guide for Christian Discipleship and Mentoring* by Wanda Bolton-Davis, 11-12. Cedar Hill, Tex.: Victorious Disciples Publishing, 2014.

Gladen, Steve. *Small Groups with Purpose: How to Create Healthy Communities*. Grand Rapids: Baker Books, 2013.

Henry, Matthew. *Matthew Henry's Commentary on the Whole Bible: Complete and Unabridged in One Volume*. Peabody, Mass: Hendrickson, 1994.

Hull, Bill. *Jesus Christ, Disciplemaker*. Grand Rapids: Baker, 2004.

_____. *The Complete Book of Discipleship: On Being and Making Followers of Christ*. Colorado Springs: NavPress, 2006.

_____. *The Disciple-Making Church*. Grand Rapids: Baker, 1990.

LifeWay, "Spiritual Growth Assessment." Accessed June 14, 2012. http://www.lifeway.com/lwc/files/lwcF_PDF_DSC_Spiritual_Growth_Assessment.pdf.

Lunde, Jonathan. *Following Jesus, the Servant King: A Biblical Theology of Covenantal Discipleship*. Grand Rapids: Zondervan, 2010.

McDonald, Glen. *The Disciple-Making Church: From Dry Bones to Spiritual Vitality*. Lima, Ohio: FaithWalk, 2007.

Mosley, Eddie. *Connecting in Communities: Understanding the Dynamics of Small Groups*. Colorado Springs: Nav Press, 2011.

Munroe, Myles. *Applying the Kingdom: Rediscovering the Priority of God for Mankind*. Shippensburg, Penn: Destiny Image, 2007.

Ogden, Greg. *Transforming Discipleship: Making Disciples a Few at a Time*. Downers Grove, Ill.: InterVarsity, 2003.

Pavao, Paul, "The Council of Nicea: Part III." *Christian History for Everyman*. Accessed October 16, 2014, http://www.christian-history.org/council-of-nicea-3.html.

Petersen, Jim. *Lifestyle Discipleship: The Challenge of Following Jesus in Today's World*. Colorado Springs: NavPress, 1993.

Putman, Jim, Bobby Harrington, and Robert E. Coleman. *Disciple Shift: Five Steps That Help Your Church Make Disciples That Make Disciples*. Grand Rapids: Zondervan, 2013.

Redford, Douglas. *The New Testament Church: Acts-Revelation*. Cincinnati: Stand Publishing, 2007.

Richey, Katherine. "Number of Muslims Worldwide Expected to Nearly Equal Number of Christians by 2050; Religiously Unaffiliated Will Make Up Declining Share of World's Population," *Pew Forum* (April 2, 2015). Accessed August 25, 2019. https://www.pewforum.org/2015/04/02/number-of-muslims-worldwide-expected-to-nearly-equal-number-of-christians-by-2050-religiously-unaffiliated-will-make-up-declining-share-of-worlds-population/.

Scazzero, Peter. *The Emotionally Healthy Church: A Strategy for Discipleship that Actually Changes Lives*. Grand Rapids: Zondervan, 2003.

Turner, M. and G. McFarlane. "Trinity." *New Bible Dictionary*, 3rd ed. Ed by D. R. W. Wood, et al. Downers Grove, Ill.: InterVarsity Press, 1996.

William G. Rusch, ed. *The Trinitarian Controversy: Sources of Early Christian Thought*. Philadelphia: Fortress Press, 1980.

Wright, Christopher. *Mission of God: Unlocking the Bible's Grand Narrative*. Downers Grove, Ill.: InterVarsity, 2006.

Smith, Barry D. "Summary of Dead Sea Scrolls," section 3. *Crandall University Professor Pages*. Accessed September 10, 2014. http://www.mycrandall.ca/courses/NTIntro/InTest/Qumran.htm#Q3.

Spence, H. D. M., and Joseph S. Exell. *The Pulpit Commentary*. 1919. Reprint, Peabody, Mass.: Hendrickson, 1985.

Spickard, Paul R. and Kevin M. Cragg. *A Global History of Christians: How Everyday Believers Experienced Their World*. Grand Rapids: Baker Academic, 1994.

Stanley, Andy and Bill Willits. *Creating Community: 5 Keys to Building a Small Group Culture*. Colorado Springs: Multnomah Books, 2004.

Webber, Robert E. *Ancient-Future Evangelism: Making Our Church a Faith-Forming Community*. Grand Rapids: Baker Books, 2003.

Michael Wilkins. *Discipleship in the Ancient World and Matthew's Gospel*. Grand Rapids: Baker Books, 1995.

_____. *Following the Master: A Biblical Theology of Discipleship*. Grand Rapids: Zondervan, 1992.

Willard, Dallas. *The Great Omission*. New York: Harper Collins, 2006.

West, Kenneth S. *Wuest's Word Studies from the Greek New Testament: For the English Reader*. Grand Rapids: Eerdmans, 1997. Logos Bible Software.

Made in the USA
Monee, IL
25 February 2024